Creative Health Inst

~ Presents ~

EATING RAW, LIVING WELL

by

HIAWATHA CROMER

Hiawatha Cromer developed these recipes while serving as director, instructor and kitchen manager at the Creative Health Institute (CHI) from 1993 to 2001, and with The Assembly of Yahweh Wellness Center, beginning in 2001.
Some recipes were created by participants in the program; a few have come from other sources.

Copyright © 2020 by Hiawatha Cromer

7911 Columbia Hwy. • Eaton Rapids, MI 48909 • 517-663-1637

All rights reserved. This book or any portion thereof may not be reproduced or transmitted in any form or manner, electronic or mechanical, including photocopying, recording, or by any information storage or retrieval system, without the express written permission of the copyright owner except for the use of brief quotations in a book review or other noncommercial uses permitted by copyright law.

Printed in the United States of America

Library of Congress Control Number:	2020909847
ISBN: Softcover	978-1-64908-213-8
eBook	978-1-64908-212-1

Republished by: PageTurner Press and Media LLC
Publication Date: 06/01/2020

To order copies of this book, contact:

PageTurner Press and Media
Phone: 1-888-447-9651
order@pageturner.us
www.pageturner.us

EATING RAW, LIVING WELL

by

HIAWATHA CROMER

Contents

Acknowledgments x
My Journey to Wellness xi
What is Living Food? 1
Breakfast 2
    Oatmeal 3
    Apple Sauce 4
    Sesame Banana Smoothie 5
    Banana Republic 6
    Mango Tango 7
    Two-Way Cantaloupe 8
    Miss Figgy Pear 9
    Apple Celery Smoothie 10
    Apple Fig Smoothie 11
    Vanilla Pears 12
    Banana Carob Smoothie 13
    Apple Beet Smoothie 14
    Apple Banana Millet Smoothie 15
    Prune Supreme 16
    Smoother Mover 17
Herbs That are Beneficial for Health 18
Soups 19
    Why Blended Soup? 20
    Dr. Ann's Energy Soup 22
    Warm Vegetable Soup 23
    Cucumber Energy Soup 24
    Cabbage Soup 25
    Broccoli Energy Soup 26

v

Blending for Better Digestion	27
Salads	***28***
Relish the Corn	30
Arame-Sesame Salad	32
Carrot-Raisin Supreme	33
Carrot-Raisin-Coconut Salad	35
Cole Slaw	36
Repeat the Beet	37
Beet-Sauerkraut	38
Cucumber-Wakame	39
Radish-Parsley Patch	40
Collard Green Salad	41
Marinated Vegetable Salad	42
Marinated Sprouts	44
Oriental Turnip Salad	46
Green Bean-Wakame Salad	47
Mock Red Salmon	48
Nori Rolls	49
Mock Potato Salad	50
Sauerkraut	51
Hummus	53
Veggie Tuna	54
Cucumber Serenade	55
Onion Relish	56
Cranberry Sauce	57
Apple Blossom Salad	58
Raw foods are the most nutritious – what is the next best thing?	59
Salad Dressings	***60***
Miso-Tahini Dressing	61
Pumpkin Seed Dressing	62
Corn-Avocado	63
Mock Thousand Island Dressing	64
French-Style Salad Dressing	65
Sesame-Garlic Dressing	66
Live Green Goddess-Spanish	68
Oil & Vinegar Dressing	69
Mock Thousand Island Dressing #2	70

Beet-Sunflower Seed Dressing 71
Miso-Nayonaise Dressing 72
Cranberry Sauce 73
Garlic Dressing 74
Cucumber-Avocado Dressing 75
Tomato Dressing 76
The Supreme Machine!! 77

Desserts and Snacks **78**
Various Snacks 79
Carrot Cake with Almond Icing 80
Sweet Potato Pie #1 81
Sweet Potato Pie #2 83
Apple Pie 85
Banana Cream Pudding 87
Banana Ice Cream 89
Victoria's Secret 90
Frankie's Cookies 91
Balancing Live Foods 93
Proteins 95
Mock Turkey 96
Seed Cheese 97
Almond Crème 98
Sesame Milk 99
Almond Cabbage Loaf 100
Sunflower Seed Loaf 101
Holiday Dressing 102
Sunflower-Sesame Seed Cheese 103
Nancy's Almond Loaf 105

Most Dangerous Foods 106
Dehydrated Foods ***107***
Dehydrated Bananas 108
Protein Nuggets 109
Bread Replacements 109
Basic Bread 109
Grain Crisps 110
George's Crackers – Papadam Style 111
Everybody's Favorite Crackers 112

    Garden Burgers 113
    Banana-Nut Pancakes 115
Five Basic Rules of Food Combining *117*
Miscellaneous Recipes **118**
    Gwen's Pizza 120
    Noor's Recipes 123
    Breakfast Tart With Banana Sauce 124
    Tabouli 126
    Squash Royale Energy Soup 127
    Hiawatha's & Lou's Barley Bread and Sandwich Spread 128
    Fig & Papaya Anti Aging Salad 129
    Hiawatha's Awesome Sesame Garlic Dressing 132
    Hiawatha's Cabbage Salad 133
    Yummy Italian Dressing 134
    Apple Pie 135
    Lasagna – Victoria's Recipe 136
    Caroline's Supreme Sunflower Seed Paté 138
    Jade's Seed Cheese (non-fermented) 139
    Jade's Fabulous Hummus 140
    Raw Cream of Broccoli Soup 141
    Nori Rolls 142
    Arame Cabbage Marinade 144
    Avocado Dressing 145
    Maxine's Natural French Dressing 146
    Oatmeal 147
    Cashew Crème 148
    Almond Crème 149
    Cleopatra Carrot Cake 150
    Queen Elinor Cream Frosting 151
    Banana/Coconut/Tahini Cream Pie* 152
    Cranberry Salad 154
    Mother Knows Best Salad 155
    Jade's Sensuous Salmon 156
    Sweet Onion Relish 157
Spice It Up!!! *158*
How to Sprout 159
Rejuvelac (How to Make) 163

Health Benefits of Some Vegetables Used With Raw/Living Foods 165
Living Foods Milk Alternatives 167
    Dr. Ann Wigmore's Nut and Seed Milk 170
    Dr. Ann's Wheat Milk 172
    Malted Wheat Milk 173
The Benefits of Raw/ Living Foods 174
Having a "Natural" Ball at Holiday Times or Special Occasions 175
Menu Planning Guidelines 176
Raw Foods and the Biggest Myth Ever 177
Resources 181

Acknowledgments

Many thanks to

Dee Lyons for her typesetting, layout and editing assistance;

Caroline Carriere and Billye Graham for their help in compiling some of the instruction guidelines;

and the many participants at the Creative Health Institute and
the Assembly of Yahweh Wellness Center
for their enthusiastic support and encouragement during the compilation of
the *Eating Raw: Living Well* recipe book.

My Journey to Wellness

In April 1993, I was suffering much discomfort in my right leg, to the extent that I was considering the use of a cane, and I weighed 220 pounds, which probably contributed to the pain in my leg. I knew I needed help, so I visited Creative Health Institute (CHI) and was told that a kitchen manager was needed. I resigned my position with the Single Parent Family Institute in Lansing, Michigan, and reported for duty at CHI on May 1, 1993 (a date I will never forget).

This was the turning point in my life. I had, in the past, tried numerous diets in an attempt to control my weight, none of which were successful. From May 1, 1993 until February 1994, I did not eat any cooked food.

My daily food intake consisted of three servings of wheatgrass juice, sunflower and buckwheat greens, lightly fermented foods (seed cheese, sauerkraut and rejuvelac), fruits and vegetables, sprouts and soaked nuts. Additionally, I took daily wheatgrass implants.

During this time, Mary Haughey provided me with guidance in learning and practicing Creative Health Institute living foods program. Whenever I left the Institute to visit friends, I always carried my food with me and avoided restaurants. By February 1994, I had lost 60 pounds, the pain in my right leg was gone, my biannual bout with sinus infection had been eliminated, and my energy level had increased. I was added to the payroll at CHI and was elevated to program director, a position that I held intermittently until March 2001.

I owe a debt of gratitude to Donald Haughey, founder of CHI, who provided the opportunity to learn, practice and teach Creative Health Institute's Living Foods Program.

What is Living Food?

Why is it necessary to incorporate living foods in one's life?

Living food is nourishment that is easy to digest. This nourishment is provided through the use of seeds, nuts, grains, fruits and vegetables, prepared by various techniques that are simple and inexpensive. These include blending, fermentation and the use of sprouting and growing greens indoors. Living food is an energy provider that has the ability to do two things: First, it cleanses the body of toxins that have accumulated through our lifetime from a poor education and misunderstanding of quality nutrition as well as from poor eating habits and environmental factors. The second ability of living foods is to rebuild our body in a natural way, thus returning to the quality of life our Creator intended for all to enjoy — total health and well-being.

Nourishment that is easy to digest also strengthens the immune system against various hazardous conditions that we cannot avoid being exposed to such as acid rain, ozone conditions, lead pollution from automobiles, and extreme heat that promotes the multiplication and mutation of dangerous germs from unhealthy environments.

Living food provides the body's cells with nourishment for self-healing.

Living foods help one reconnect with nature and creates a confidence and self- responsibility for one's own life. By adopting a healthy lifestyle, one can experience a sense of freedom from addictions of various sorts — food, drugs, alcohol and sex — with which our society now suffers due to various unbalanced states of body and mind.

Eating raw and living foods replaces the present, deteriorating health and mind conditions that are currently termed "incurable" with important, energy- giving nourishment for building health and self respect.

Breakfast

Contents

Oatmeal 3
Apple Sauce 4
Sesame Banana Smoothie 5
Banana Republic 6
Mango Tango 7
Two-Way Cantaloupe 8
Miss Figgy Pear 9
Apple Celery Smoothie 10
Apple Fig Smoothie 11
Vanilla Pears 12
Banana Carob Smoothie 13
Apple Beet Smoothie 14
Apple Banana Millet Smoothie 15
Prune Supreme 16
Smoother Mover 17

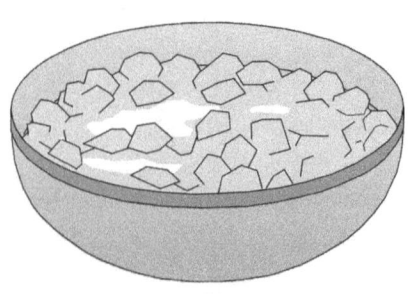

Oatmeal

Ingredients

¼ cup old-fashioned oatmeal
1 cup apple juice
⅛ cup walnuts
⅛ cup coconut (fine shredded, dry or fresh)
⅛ cup raisins
2-5 Tbsp. ground flax seed

To Prepare

Soak old-fashioned oats overnight in one cup of apple juice. Soak walnuts, coconut and raisins in water. Soak separately. Discard the water from soaking nuts. Use water from coconuts and raisins.

Serves one to two people.

Health Benefits

- Lowers cholesterol levels, if a problem. Very filling.
- Helps to regulate bowels.
- Flax seeds add Omega 3 and Omega 6 fatty acids, which are essential fatty acids.
- Raisins add alkalinity.

Apple Sauce

Ingredients

4 apples (Braeburn) crisp; not discolored
1 mango
bananas
½ cup currants 1 lemon, juiced

To Prepare

Soak currants overnight. Wash and dice apples, peel and dice mango, peel and slice bananas. Place these ingredients in a mixing bowl. Add currants and lemon juice. Mix slightly. Will keep for 2-3 days in refrigerator.

Health Benefits

- Apple — pectin
- Currants — alkaline
- Bananas — potassium
- Mango — beta carotene
- Very cleansing
- Very satisfying for a sweet tooth.

Sesame Banana Smoothie

Ingredients

cups sesame milk
5-6 frozen bananas
1 tsp. carob powder (optional)

To Prepare

Blend one cup of sesame seeds with four cups of water to make sesame milk. Strain (separate milk and pulp). Add bananas and carob to milk. Blend thoroughly.

To make a heavy breakfast, add ¼ to a cup of oat groats (soaked overnight) per person with the bananas before blending.

Health Benefits

- High in calcium and potassium.

Banana Republic

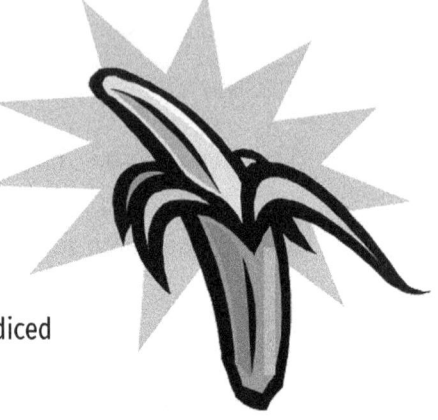

Ingredients

½ cup prunes
½ cup dates
cup seedless raisins
3 cups water
bananas, peeled and diced
1 tsp. almond extract

To Prepare

Soak raisins, prunes and dates overnight in one cup water. Combine all fruit; add 1 tsp. almond extract; pour over two peeled, sliced bananas.

When serving, sprinkle one tablespoon of ground flax seed on top of each individual serving.

Health Benefits

- This is a cleansing, sweet treat that will satisfy one's desire for desserts.
- Flax seeds provide essential fatty acids, which the body does not manufacture. You must get essential fatty acids from your diet.

Mango Tango

Ingredients

    2 mangoes
    2 cups sprouted mung beans
    2 apples blended with water to cover
    1 lemon, juiced

To Prepare

    Sprout mung beans until tail appears (see sprouting instructions). Peel and dice mangoes. Add to mung bean sprouts. Blend apples with water and lemon juice; pour over mung sprouts and mangoes.

Health Benefits

- Mung beans have a high amount of protein. Mangoes are high in beta carotene.

Two-Way Cantaloupe

Ingredients

1 cantaloupe (keep seeds)
1 avocado
½ tsp. nutmeg
½ tsp. cardamon

o Prepare

Cut open cantaloupe. Save the seeds and membrane. Blend seeds and membrane with ½ cup water. Strain and save liquor

Discard the seeds. Dice cantaloupe and place in a bowl. Dice avocado and pour cantaloupe liquor over the pieces. Sprinkle with nutmeg and cardamon.

Can be served as a smoothie. Blend all ingredients. Serve in glasses.

Health Benefits

- Beta Carotene
- Cleansing

Miss Figgy Pear

Ingredients

6 figs (Calimyrna or black mission), soaked
4 pears, diced
1 tsp. vanilla
1 lemon, juiced

To Prepare

Soak figs overnight in one cup water. Core and dice pears. Use soaking water to blend pears and figs. Add lemon juice and vanilla.

Health Benefits

- Pears — potassium
- Good drink for constipation.

Apple Celery Smoothie

Ingredients

2 apples
1 stalk celery
½ avocado
1 cup water
¼ tsp. nutmeg

To Prepare

Wash and core apples. Quarter apples. Cut celery in one-inch pieces. Place in blender with one cup of water. Add avocado. Blend until smooth. Pour into a bowl and sprinkle nutmeg on top to decorate.

This is a serving for one person.

Health Benefits

- Helps with sodium/potassium balance.
- Calms the nerves.
- Curbs the desire for sweets.

Apple Fig Smoothie

Ingredients

2 apples per person
3 figs per person (soaked with soaking water)
¼ cup old-fashioned oats
¼ cup water
Dash of cinnamon

To Prepare

Place all ingredients together in a blender and mix until smooth.

Health Benefits

- Provides minerals.
- Good for skin, hair and fingernails.
- Provides pectin, which absorbs and dissolves toxins and stimulates peristaltic activity.
- Helps with elimination.

Vanilla Pears

Ingredients

4 fresh pears, halved and cored
2 bananas
1 cup water
2 tsp. vanilla
2 Tbsp. powdered agar agar

To Prepare

Place halved, cored pears in a shallow dish.

Bring water and agar agar to a boil, let boil for five minutes until agar agar is dissolved; cool. Add vanilla and blend with bananas and water. Pour mixture over pears. Let set before serving.

Serves four. Serve this dish as a breakfast treat or dessert. Top with 1 Tbsp. of Almond Crème (page 84).

Health Benefits

- Fruits are cleansing and help with elimination.
- The agar agar adds minerals and is soothing for the intestinal tract.

Banana Carob Smoothie

(summer dessert or breakfast)

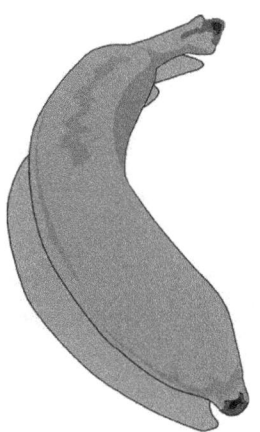

Ingredients

4-5 bananas, frozen
1 tsp. carob powder
3 cups water

To Prepare

Blend above ingredients thoroughly.

In-season options: banana/blueberry; banana/strawberry

Can be used for breakfast or as a dessert. When using as breakfast recipe, blend with sesame milk and add ¼ cup of old-fashioned oats per person.

Health Benefits

- High in potassium.

Apple Beet Smoothie

Ingredients

2 apples per person
½ beet per person
½ avocado per person or ¼ cup soaked flax seeds
1 cup pure water per person
½ lemon, juiced

To Prepare

Wash and core applies. Cut in quarters and place in blender with water.

Wash beets, dice and add to above. Blend until smooth, add avocado or flax and lemon juice. Blend and serve immediately.

Health Benefits

- This dish is helpful to detoxify the liver.

Apple Banana Millet Smoothie

Ingredients

½ cup of millet (soaked overnight) 2 bananas
2 apples
2 cups water (use the millet water) 2 Tbsp. maple syrup (optional)
1 tsp. pure vanilla
½ tsp. ground cardamon
¼ cup soaked raisins (for topping)

To Prepare

Wash millet three times. Pour water off millet with a strainer to avoid wasting seeds. Cover with 2 cups of pure water. Soak overnight in refrigerator. Wash bananas before peeling to get rid of any insect eggs. Wash apples and core. Use peeling if organic. Blend all ingredients except raisins. Sprinkle raisins on top to serve.

Health Benefits

- Helps with acid/alkaline balance of the body. Serve often.

Prune Supreme

Ingredients

4 prunes soaked in ½ cup water per person
¼ cup oat bran soaked in ½ cup water per person
2 Tbsp. ground flax seeds per person
½ tsp. nutmeg
½ Tbsp. cinnamon
½ tsp. cardamon

To Prepare

Wash and soak prunes overnight in refrigerator. Soak oat bran overnight in refrigerator. Be sure to remove pit from prunes.

Add remaining ingredients and blend.

Health Benefits

- This dish is excellent for people who have problems with elimination. Flax seed is nature's richest source of essential fatty acids, which you must get from your diet, for the body does not manufacture them.
- Other sources of essential fatty acids are fish, soybeans, green leafy vegetables, nuts, and seeds.
- Many dieters claim that flax seeds help them to lose unwanted body fat.

Smoother Mover

Ingredients

2 Tbsp. oat bran
2 Tbsp. flax seed meal (ground up flax seeds)
2 Tbsp. oatmeal
2 Tbsp. wheat germ
½ tsp. kelp
¼ cup raisins
1 Tbsp. sunflower seeds
1 banana, sliced or apple, grated
1 cup apple juice or water if you need to reduce sugar intake

To Prepare

Combine all ingredients except banana or apple and soak overnight in liquid in refrigerator. Next morning, add sliced banana or grated apple before eating.

Health Benefits

- Fiber helps with elimination. Be sure to drink two glasses of water before each meal, minimal six glasses per day unless you are drinking a glass of freshly extracted juices two or more times per day.

Herbs That are Beneficial for Health

Basil	Sweet and mild flavored. Use ¼ to ½ tsp. for four people. Leaves can be used fresh in salads, in energy soup or chopped and added to dressings. Good with tomatoes and peas.
Caraway Seeds	Good for digestion. Similar to anise. Can be used in soups and vegetables, especially to season red cabbage.
Cayenne	Good for digestion, circulation, and to provide a warming effect in the winter.
Coriander	Sweet and tart. This herb is mentioned in the Scriptures. Use in soups. It is one of the ingredients in curry.
Chives	Mild antibiotic, stimulates the appetite and strengthens the stomach. Good for the kidneys and helps to keep blood pressure down. Use chopped in salads. One teaspoon is enough to serve four people.
Chervil	Similar to parsley, but sweeter. Flavors salads, cleans the blood and helps the kidneys. Grows best in semi-shaded areas. Use one teaspoon for two people. Good for cold soups. Refreshing and aromatic.
Clove	Aids digestion. Use in pea soup.
Dill	Rich in minerals. Use dill weed in salads. Use seeds in hot vegetables.

For descriptions of The Assembly of Yahweh Wellness Center, visit www.assemblyofyahweh.com/living.htm.

Soups

Energy Soups —

    Fruits only
    Vegetables only
    Mixed

Why Blended Soup? 20

Dr. Ann's Energy Soup 22

Warm Vegetable Soup 23

Cucumber Energy Soup 24

Cabbage Soup 25

Broccoli Energy Soup 26

Why Blended Soup?

By Dr. Ann Wigmore

The key is that it works! Energy soup gives the body's cells fuel to be nourished, which provides the means for self-healing. Another reason that this energy soup is high energy nourishment is that it is fermented slightly from the blending with rejuvelac, which starts the breakdown of nutrients into usable forms.

This soup provides a complete form of basic elements that are needed for healing by blending a variety of foods that are easy to digest, assimilate and eliminate from the body. Since most of the essential elements are missing from our chemicalized, devitalized and industrialized food products and produce, providing a variety of easy-to-digest essential nutrients is important in the rejuvenation of the body. The elements that are missing in "regular food," of course, have, for many, upset the body and mind. Addictions to negative behaviors and habits are good examples of an upset body/mind. This is also true for many other health problems that people suffer with every day, which generally have been brought on by overeating and chemicalization in growing, preserving, processing, and/or preparing.

Energy soup (the high-energy nourishment) should be taken about five times per day in small amounts (one cup or less per serving). For variety, you can add one-half cut-up banana or some alfalfa sprouts as topping for the energy soup so there is something to chew. Chewing is important so that the food mixes with the saliva and the body can begin the digestive process.

The most important health builders are high-energy nourishment from energy soup, rejuvelac and wheatgrass, which can be taken before eating energy soup or when hungry.

Energy Soup

Included is a sample of recipes for energy soup. We want readers to be creative in developing their own by using the following guidelines.

Blend three or more vegetables and sprouts with vegetable juice, fruit juice or water. Add lemon juice, herbs for seasoning, an avocado and dulse or kelp for minerals. Bragg's Aminos or tamari may also be added. The flavor can be varied according to the vegetables used.

People who are not diabetic and who like sweetness can blend a variety of properly combined fruits with lemon juice and avocado. Diabetics should use vegetable juices for liquid.

Dr. Ann's Energy Soup

Ingredients

1 apple or pear (or 1 cup diced watermelon)
1 tsp. dulse (or kelp or nori for minerals)
1 cup rejuvelac (see page 127) or water or vegetable juice
1 cup alfalfa sprouts or assorted sprouts, such as lentils, mung beans, chick peas, etc. (optional)
2-3 cups buckwheat sprouts, cleaned
½ avocado
½ lemon, juiced
1 tsp. Bragg's Aminos (optional)

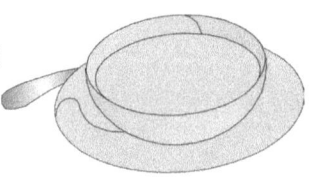

To Prepare

Blend together until smooth, adding avocado last. Adjust ingredients to taste.

Serves one or two people.

Health Benefits

- A good source of chlorophyll, enzymes, b-complex vitamins, vitamin C, beta carotene, iodine and other trace minerals.
- According to Dr. Andrew Weil, alfalfa sprouts contain a toxic substance. Therefore, I suggest that people with weak immune systems avoid alfalfa sprouts.

Warm Vegetable Soup

Ingredients

1 small cucumber (use seed)

1 small green pepper or ½ of large green pepper (use seeds)

⅛ head of cabbage

1 medium tomato

1 tsp. white miso

1 cup warm water

To Prepare

To make dish: Cut up vegetables in large chunks. Place in blender with one cup warm water (use cooking thermometer; do not heat over 120° F) and one tsp. white miso. Blend for two minutes or until the desired consistency.

Eat Immediately. Serves two to four.

Health Benefits

- Cucumbers contain silicon for hair, nails and skin.
- Green pepper has chlorophyll, and seeds contain vitamin E, a powerful antioxidant.
- Tomatoes contain vitamin C.
- Miso has enzymes.

Cucumber Energy Soup

Ingredients

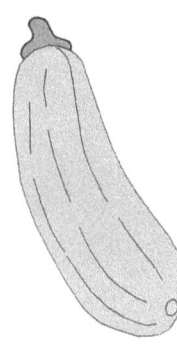

2 medium cucumbers (peel if not organic)
2 large tomatoes
1 cup sprouted green peas (sprout only 2 days)
1 Tbsp. ground dulse
1 Tbsp. Bragg's Aminos
1 clove of garlic, minced
1 cup greens (sunflower or buckwheat) or other green vegetables
water if necessary

To Prepare

Blend ingredients in the order listed.

Health Benefits

- A good source of silicon, sulfur and trace elements; a beautifier for the hair and nails.
- Will cool the body during hot weather.

Cabbage Soup

Ingredients

½ head of small cabbage
1 small carrot
¼ green pepper or red pepper
¼ onion
1 clove garlic
1 Tbsp. kelp
2 cups water
1 avocado
¼ fennel seed (ground)
¼ tsp. caraway seeds Bragg's Aminos to taste

To Prepare

Blend first six ingredients with water; add avocado, caraway seeds and Bragg's. Blend until desired smoothness is attained.

Health Benefits

- Excellent for people with stomach problems and problems with elimination.

Broccoli Energy Soup

Ingredients

2 cups sesame milk (see page 85)
2 cups raw broccoli
1 small onion
dill weed to taste
Bragg's Aminos to taste

To Prepare

Blend ingredients until desired consistency.

Health Benefits

- Broccoli is a member of the cruciferous family, which is known to prevent cancer. A cruciferous vegetable should be eaten daily (broccoli, cabbage, Brussels sprouts, cauliflower, etc.).
- Broccoli is also rich in vitamins and minerals.

Blending for Better Digestion

Because of the severe digestive problems that 90% of us are facing as a population, it is imperative we have means to help our body assimilate nourishment.

Blending is a fabulous solution for our digestive problems.

Blending is the easiest and most efficient way to provide food that is both nourishing and easy to digest. By blending foods, we can counteract the poor eating habits most of us have developed over the years; habits that are the cause of many of the physical problems we have.

It has long been known that what we eat directly affects our health. The average American diet consists mainly of processed foods that are high in fat, cholesterol, salt and sugar, and low in fresh fruits and vegetables and whole grains. Eventually, this type of intake leads to digestive troubles, obesity, heart disease and cancer, as well as nutritional deficiencies that cause a host of problems of their own.

Blending is equally appropriate for people who are ill and people who are healthy. If you are ill, blending your food will relieve your body of some extra efforts required for digestion, so this energy may be better spent on healing.

Blending with rejuvelac prevents the loss of vitamins because the high vitamin E content in rejuvelac acts as an anti-oxidant. Blending is a means to help us chew our food in order to make it digestible because no amount of chewing can really provide us with the level of digestibility as does blending, especially when blending with rejuvelac, which contains a very high level of enzymes.

Blending reduces the need for food combining, since the food becomes pre-digested.

Salads

Relish the Corn	30
Arame-Sesame Salad	32
Carrot-Raisin Supreme	33
Carrot-Raisin-Coconut Salad	35
Cole Slaw	36
Repeat the Beet	37
Beet-Sauerkraut	38
Cucumber-Wakame	39
Radish-Parsley Patch	40
Collard Green Salad	41
Marinated Vegetable Salad	42
Marinated Sprouts	44
Oriental Turnip Salad	46
Green Bean-Wakame Salad	47
Mock Red Salmon	48
Nori Rolls	49
Mock Potato Salad	50
Sauerkraut	51
Hummus	53

Veggie Tuna *54*
Cucumber Serenade *55*
Onion Relish *56*
Cranberry Sauce *57*
Apple Blossom Salad *58*

Relish the Corn

Ingredients

8 to 10 ears corn, cut off the cob
1 large onion, sliced
1 yellow summer squash, diced
1 stalk celery, diced
1-2 red peppers, diced
1 cucumber, seeded and diced (peeled if skin is tough)
(clean out cucumber; keep it fresh; very digestible once seeds are removed)

<u>Sauce</u>
1 avocado, mashed
3-5 cloves garlic, minced
1-2 lemons, juiced
1 Tbsp. Bragg's Aminos to taste tomatoes or 1 cup water
1 tsp. chives, minced
¼ tsp. dill weed

To Prepare

Mix the first six ingredients lightly. In separate bowl, mix next six ingredients and add to first bowl; mix well to coat all the vegetables.

or —

Refrigerate each mixture separately and mix individually when served.

Health Benefits

- Corn provides fiber and beta carotene.
- People with digestive problems should blend the salad mixtures.

Arame-Sesame Salad

Ingredients

2 cups arame
¼ cup white sesame seeds, ground
1 tomato or medium red pepper, diced
1 small onion, diced
1 lemon, juiced
1 tsp. Bragg's Aminos

To Prepare

Soak arame for five minutes. Grind sesame seeds in coffee grinder.

Combine ingredients and serve. Will keep 3 days.

Health Benefits

- Arame is a sea vegetable, high in sodium and minerals. Sesame seeds are high in calcium
- Tomatoes are high in vitamin C, and are blood cleansers; good for skin, liver and gall bladder.
- Not recommended in cases of cancer.

Carrot-Raisin Supreme

Ingredients

4 carrots, grated
½ cup raisins
¼ cup powdered coconut (optional) 1 apple, diced
2 lemons, juiced
1 Tbsp. maple syrup

To Prepare

Grate carrots in food processor. Soak raisins in ½ cup water. Add remaining ingredients. Let set at least two hours before serving.

Will keep up to three days in refrigerator.

This recipe can be used to make a carrot cake; however, carrots have to be put through Champion with the blank.

Health Benefits

- Carrots are high in vitamin A and a full range of minerals. Good for eyes, hair, skin and provides energy.
- Raisins are alkaline; therefore, helpful with body's pH balance.

- Coconut is useful in cases of liver trouble, digestive problems and nervousness. It is high in fat, carbohydrate and protein.
- Apples are cleansers of the digestive tract. They contain silicon and pectin. Good for hair, skin and fingernails.
- Lemon is a source of vitamins C and A. Good for colds.
- Maple syrup is more gentle on the pancreas than white sugar or honey.

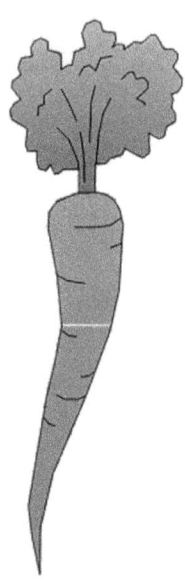

Carrot-Raisin-Coconut Salad

Ingredients

4 carrots
1 cup raisins (save ½ cup to decorate)
½ cup unsweetened coconut (finely grated; purchase at health- food store)
½ cup walnuts, soaked and chopped coarsely
1 lemon, juiced and seeded
½ tsp. allspice or cinnamon or nutmeg
1 tsp. pure vanilla flavoring

To Prepare

Juice carrots, then combine the juice and pulp. Add remaining ingredients. Decorate with ½ cup raisins.

Salad will keep three to four days.

Health Benefits

- Carrots contain beta carotene; good for eyesight. Coconut provides bulk for colon.
- Raisins help to alkalize the body to bring it into proper acid/alkaline balance.

Cole Slaw

Ingredients

¼ large green cabbage or ½ small cabbage
1 carrot
¼ green pepper
1 stalk celery
1 small onion
1 tsp. caraway seeds
4 Tbsp. nayonaise (purchase at health-food store; has less fat than mayonnaise)
1 lemon, juiced

To Prepare

Chop cabbage in food processor. Chop carrot in food processor. Dice green pepper, celery and onions. Add caraway seeds, nayonaise and lemon juice and toss.

Health Benefits

- Cabbage is good for the stomach, contains vitamins U, C and A. It also contains practically all the minerals.
- Green pepper contains fluorine and silicon, which is good for hair, skin, nails. Also contains vitamin C. The seeds contain vitamin E.
- Celery dissolves calcium deposits and is highly alkaline, therefore valuable for correcting inflammation of urinary tract.

Repeat the Beet

Ingredients

4 medium beets
1 lemon, juiced
1 Tbsp. honey or maple syrup
1 tsp. mint leaves, fresh or dry (or peppermint tea leaves in bulk)

To Prepare

Put beets through food processor or Champion with blank. Add lemon, honey and mint.

Keeps well.

Health Benefits

- Lemon and honey balance pH. Mint — digestion.
- Beets — blood tonic.

Beet-Sauerkraut

Ingredients

4 beets
1 cup sauerkraut (preferably homemade)
1 green pepper, diced
1 clove garlic, minced

To Prepare

Put beets through food processor or Champion juicer with blank. Add remaining ingredients and mix together.

Preserves well.

Health Benefits

- Beets are good for blood and liver.
- Cabbage cleanses.
- Garlic is good for blood pressure, parasites, cholesterol.
- Green pepper helps the skin, hair, nails, etc.

Cucumber-Wakame

Ingredients

2 cucumbers, peeled, seeded and sliced thinly
⅛ cup of diced wakame
½ small onion, sliced thinly
1 lemon, juiced
1 Tbsp. Bragg's Aminos
1 Tbsp. olive oil (optional)
1 tsp. thyme
1 tsp. basil

To Prepare

Peel, grate and remove seeds from cucumbers; slice thinly. Soak wakame for 10 minutes and drain. Slice onion thinly after cutting in quarters. Combine all ingredients and toss.

Will keep 3 days.

Health Benefits

- Cucumbers are high in silicon and fluorine, which is essential to the health of the skin, hair and fingernails.
- Also good for high blood pressure, hardening of the arteries, arthritis, gall stones and kidney stones.

Radish-Parsley Patch

Ingredients

2 cups parsley
1 bunch of radishes with greens
1 lemon, juiced
1 Tbsp. Bragg's Aminos
1 Tbsp. olive oil
1 tsp. tarragon
1 tsp. thyme

To Prepare

Wash radishes and greens. Cut up greens finely. Slice radish roots thinly. Combine all ingredients. Let set two hours.

Health Benefits

- Radish is a good source of iodine; helpful in dissolving mucous.
- <u>DO NOT USE</u> for arthritis, rheumatic conditions, gall stones, kidney stones or any skin conditions.

Collard Green Salad

Ingredients

1 bunch of collards (kale or any leafy greens can be substituted for the collards)
1 medium red onion
1 clove garlic
1 lemon, juiced and seeded
1 tsp. basil
1 tsp. celery seed
1 Tbsp. flax seed oil or cold-pressed, extra virgin olive oil
½ cup carrots (to add hint of sweetness)

To Prepare

Cut collards in thin slices, as thin as possible. Cut onion in half-moon shape. Mince or crush garlic. Combine all ingredients and toss to mix spices and oil. Let set at least two hours before serving. Best if marinated overnight.

Health Benefits

- Rich in calcium, minerals, chlorophyll and protein.
- Flax seed oil contains omega 3 and omega 6 oils, which help to lubricate joints and help to regulate elimination.

Marinated Vegetable Salad

Ingredients

1 medium cucumber, seeded and cubed
2 medium tomatoes, cubed
1 green pepper, sliced
⅛ small green cabbage, shredded
2 small carrots, thinly sliced
6 radishes, thinly sliced
½ onion, chopped
¼ cup lemon juice or raw apple-cider vinegar
1 Tbsp. cold-pressed olive oil
⅛ tsp. garlic powder
1 tsp. thyme
1 tsp. basil

To Prepare

Place all vegetables in a large bowl. Add lemon juice or vinegar, garlic powder and oil. Mix well. Refrigerate covered four hours or overnight.

Will keep several days.

Chopped raw broccoli, cauliflower, diced celery, sliced zucchini and chickpeas may be added.

Health Benefits

- A complete meal salad that provides a full range of vitamins and minerals.
- This salad can also be blended for easy digestibility.

Marinated Sprouts

Ingredients

1 cup lentil sprouts
1 cup mung bean sprouts
1 cup fenugreek sprouts
1 stalk celery, chopped
1 red onion, chopped
1 red pepper, chopped
1 clove garlic, minced or crushed
1 Tbsp. parsley
½ tsp. oregano
1 Tbsp. olive oil
1 lemon, juiced and seeded
1 tsp. honey
1 Tbsp. kelp
½ cup currants or 2 apples, diced

To Prepare

Mix ingredients in the manner listed. Let marinate two to four hours before serving. Refrigerate and let marinate two to four hours before serving.

Health Benefits

- This is a complete meal salad which can be blended for people with digestive problems.
- It can also be used as a salad dressing by blending and adding an avocado.
- This salad is rich in minerals.

Oriental Turnip Salad

Ingredients

1 medium Chinese turnip (purchased at oriental store)
6 jalapeno peppers (seeded)
2 Tbsp. sesame oil
1 Tbsp. Bragg's raw apple-cider vinegar
1 tsp. dill weed
1 red pepper, diced

To Prepare

Wash Chinese turnip, cut in pieces that can be put through opening in food processor with grater. Cut up six jalapeno peppers after removing seeds (the seeds are very hot, so be careful not to rub in your eyes or face while working with peppers). Add remaining ingredients and mix thoroughly.

Salad will keep three days.

Health Benefits

- Jalapeno peppers provide vitamin C. Turnip provides vitamin C and minerals.

Green Bean-Wakame Salad

Ingredients

1 cup wakame (soaked and cut into bite-size pieces)
2 cups green beans, cut at an angle roughly ¼ inch in length
1 small onion (Vidalia, Spanish, white or red)
2 Tbsp. cold-pressed, extra virgin olive oil
Bragg's Aminos to taste (about 1 Tbsp.)
1 lemon, juiced and seeded
1 tsp. ground Italian seasoning by Frontier Herbs (purchase at health food store)

To Prepare

Mix ingredients in the order listed. Salad will keep two days.

Health Benefits

- Wakame is rich in minerals.
- Green beans are especially useful for people who are diabetic; green beans nourish the pancreas.

Mock Red Salmon

Ingredients

3 cups carrot pulp
1 medium onion, chopped
1 stalk celery, chopped
2 cloves garlic, minced
½ small green pepper, chopped
1 lemon, juiced and seeded
½ cup nayonaise
1 tsp. dry parsley
1 tsp. celery seeds
1 Tbsp. Bragg's Aminos

To Prepare

Mix ingredients in the order listed. Serve on cabbage or romaine lettuce leaves.

Health Benefits

- Creative way to use carrot pulp.
- Carrots provide vitamin A and minerals.

Nori Rolls

Ingredients

3 cups soaked almonds, ground (or 3 cups seed cheese)
4 avocados, sliced thinly
1-2 cucumbers, seeded and sliced thinly
3-4 carrots, grated
3 cups alfalfa sprouts 10-15 sheets of nori

To Prepare

Dampen sheet of nori slightly with wet hand and fill one end with two tablespoons of ground almonds, two slices of avocado, two slices of cucumber, handful of sprouts and grated carrots. Roll and tuck. Moisten other end of sheet and press to hold. Cut in two pieces and serve immediately.

Health Benefits

- Provides minerals, protein; very satisfying to the appetite.

Mock Potato Salad

Ingredients

1 head of cauliflower
1 Tbsp. parsley flakes or fresh parsley
1 lemon, juiced
2 Tbsp. cold-pressed, extra virgin olive oil
1 Tbsp. Bragg's amino acid.

To Prepare

Remove leaves from cauliflower, soak head in cold water with 1 tsp. salt for 15 minutes to remove insects. Cut in pieces small enough to fit into the food processor and process until smooth. Put in mixing bowl and add remaining ingredients.

Health Benefits

- Cauliflower is one of the cruciferous vegetables that are known to prevent cancer and other degenerative diseases.

Sauerkraut

Ingredients

2 large heads of cabbage; red, white or mixed
1 beet
3-4 ground juniper berries
2-3 ounces dulse, arame, or seaweed, soaked and cut up
1 tsp. kelp (optional)
1 tsp. caraway seed, ground
1 gallon-size crock

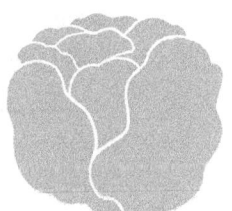

To Prepare

Shred cabbage finely. Save two to three outer cabbage leaves. Grate beet. Place cabbage and beet in a metal bowl or pail, no more than ½ full for easier pounding.

With heavy object, baseball bat, 2x4, masher, etc., pound cabbage so the fibers break down and the juice flows out, thus freeing enzymes. Pound 10-15 minutes so that each shred is translucent. The more you pound, the more of a smooth, velvety taste the sauerkraut will acquire.

Mix in spices and place in a crock, covering completely with outer cabbage leaves. Put a plate on top of the leaves and a weight, such as a brick, on top of that. Then put crock cover on and set the crock in an evenly heated (55°-75°), dark, quiet corner for six or seven days. If no crock is available, substitute a wide-mouth, preferably dark-glass jar. Tamp cabbage down, and place the outer leaves on top. Place weight on top, and cover the jar with a plastic bag and on top of that, a paper bag. (Sauerkraut ferments better in the dark.)

After a week has passed, open crock or jar. Discard outer leaves and skim residue from the top. Refrigerate. It will keep about a month.

Add sauerkraut to any salad preparation. It combines well with all vegetables and will help the body digest the meal. Blend into sauces and soups, or add in for texture and taste. Juiced, it is an unsurpassed enzyme-builder.

<u>Variations</u>

The variations in making sauerkraut are endless. Experiment with your taste buds. Use different combinations of vegetables: carrots, beets, celery, turnips, and artichokes. A favorite combination of mine is sprouted chickpeas processed with the S blade, with carrot juice to cover. Let ferment for five days.

Try different spices — thyme, dill or basil. Additions for flavor could be onions, garlic or green peppers. Remember that when making sauerkraut, do not use salt. Table salt is inorganic and often remains in the system. A better source of minerals may be found from sea vegetables such as wakame, dulse, kelp and hijiki. Unlike table salt, which is 75% sodium chloride, sea vegetables are about 18% to 20% sodium chloride.

Health Benefits

- Sauerkraut is a predigested food; starches have been broken down into simple sugars, and proteins into amino acids.
- It is a blood cleanser and helps with regular bowel movements.
- Contains much vitamin C and aids longevity through improving digestion.

Hummus

Ingredients

3 cups sprouted chickpeas
1 cup rejuvelac or pure water
½ cup raw tahini or 1 avocado
½ cup lemon juice
2 cloves garlic, minced
½ tsp. kelp
1 Tbsp. Bragg's Aminos
1 tsp. fennel (ground)

To Prepare

Blend chick peas with liquid until smooth (may need to add more liquid for desired consistency). Pour into a bowl and add remaining ingredients.

Health Benefits

- Chickpeas provide fiber, protein and enzymes.

Veggie Tuna

Ingredients

2 cups carrot pulp
½ green pepper
¼ medium onion
2 stalks celery, chopped
¼ cup nayonaise
1 Tbsp. Bragg's Aminos
1 lemon, juiced
nori sheets — optional

To Prepare

Chop green pepper, onions, celery as finely as possible. Add to carrot pulp with nayonaise, lemon juice and Bragg's. Roll in nori sheets.

Health Benefits

- Good way to use carrot pulp. Provides beta carotene and minerals.

Cucumber Serenade

Ingredients

2 cucumbers
1 small onion, sweet or red
1 lemon, juiced
1 tsp. dill weed
1 Tbsp. Bragg's Aminos

To Prepare

Remove seeds and peel cucumbers (unless burpless). Slice in half, then slice thinly. Cut onions in half moons, then quartered, then sliced thinly. Combine cucumbers and onions and lemon juice, dill weed and Bragg's. Marinate at least four hours.

Health Benefits

- Cucumbers have silicon, which is good for hair, skin and nails.
- Onions are good for heart, healthy cholesterol levels and lower blood pressure.

Onion Relish

Ingredients

6 sweet onions, sliced thin
2 lemons, juiced
2 Tbsp. honey
1 tsp. turmeric
1 tsp. dill weed

To Prepare

Mix above ingredients; let marinate for four hours. Serve with any salad or vegetable dish.

Keeps for two weeks.

Health Benefits

- Onions will help to lower cholesterol.

Cranberry Sauce

Ingredients

2 cups cored, diced apples
2 cups cranberries
½ cup maple syrup or agave or 20 drops of Stevia
½ cup pecans, chopped coarsely
1 lemon, juiced

To Prepare

Put apples and cranberries through Champion with blank. Add nuts, maple syrup and lemon juice. Let set overnight.

Health Benefits

- Cranberries are good to clean the urinary tract.
- Should be used often by people with bladder problems.

Apple Blossom Salad

Ingredients

3 gala or golden delicious apples
3 cups cauliflower
2 stalks celery
1 cup currants, soaked

Dressing
½ tsp. nutmeg and cinnamon
½ cup cashews
1 cup apple juice or apple cider or orange juice

To Prepare

Wash, core and dice apples or put through food processor. Wash and put cauliflower through food processor. Chop celery. Add currants. Blend all ingredients for dressing and pour over top. Marinate for at least one hour. Will keep for two days.

Health Benefits

- Source of organic sodium, potassium. Good for digestion and nerves.

Raw foods are the most nutritious — what is the next best thing?

Raw foods, without any question, are the most nutritious foods you could ever eat. Once foods are cooked, vitamins, minerals, enzymes and other nutrients are destroyed.

There are three factors that destroy nutrients during cooking:

1. High heat — most destructive
2. Oxidation
3. Water

Ranking of various cooking methods in order of highest to lowest nutrients:

1. **Low temperature, waterless cooking** — most nutritious cooking method. Food is never heated hotter than 220 degrees. Oxidation is practically eliminated, and water is not a problem.

2. **Steaming** — food is heated to 212 degrees, the temperature of steam. Oxidation is a big problem; vitamins and minerals are carried off with the steam. Water is also a problem because water collects at the bottom.

3. **Pressure cooking** — food is heated to over 250 degrees. Oxidation is not much of a problem because most of the steam is being pressurized and not escaping. Water is a problem because water collects at the bottom.

4. **Boiling** — food is heated to 212 degrees, the boiling point of water. Oxidation depends on the seal of the lid. It can be a big problem if no lid is on the pot. Water is a big problem. More than 50 percent of the minerals are pulled into the water. Unless the water is consumed, as in soups, this method of food preparation is not recommended because water pulls most of the flavor and nutrients out of the food.

5. **Baking and broiling** — food is heated to anywhere from 300 degrees to 600 degrees, depending on a particular recipe. This is an extremely high temperature. This is one of the worst methods of food preparation in terms of preserving nutrients.

6. **Frying** — food is heated to well over 300 degrees. Oils are heated along with the food. Heated oils should be avoided completely because they are almost impossible for the body to digest and break down. This method of cooking not only destroys most of the nutrients in the food, but it also adds toxins into the body.

Salad Dressings

Dressing Up Your Salads

Miso-Tahini Dressing 61
Pumpkin Seed Dressing 62
Corn-Avocado 63
Mock Thousand Island Dressing 64
French-Style Salad Dressing 65
Sesame-Garlic Dressing 66
Live Green Goddess-Spanish 68
Oil & Vinegar Dressing 69
Mock Thousand Island Dressing #2 70
Beet-Sunflower Seed Dressing 71
Miso-Nayonaise Dressing 72
Cranberry Sauce 73
Garlic Dressing 74
Cucumber-Avocado Dressing 75
Tomato Dressing 76

> Hint: A few drops of colloidal silver or liquid oxygen added to dressings keeps them fresh much longer.

Miso-Tahini Dressing

Ingredients

½ cup raw tahini
3 Tbsp. white miso
½ cup fresh lemon juice
½ cup distilled water

1 tsp. garlic granules
½ tsp. basil
½ tsp. thyme
½ tsp. oregano
1-2 red peppers, diced

Or: 1 ½ tsp. of ground Italian seasoning

To Prepare

Blend all ingredients just enough to mix thoroughly.

Will keep seven days.

Health Benefits

- Enzyme-rich to help digestion and assimilation.

Pumpkin Seed Dressing

Ingredients

    2 cups pumpkin seeds, soaked or ground
    2 cups water or more if needed
    2 cloves garlic, sliced
    1 small onion, sliced
    1 tsp. ground Italian seasoning
    Bragg's Aminos to taste

To Prepare

Blend all ingredients until smooth.

Health Benefits

- Provides protein and zinc.

Corn-Avocado

Ingredients

> 3 to 4 ears of corn, cut off cob
> 1 avocado
> 2 cloves garlic, crushed
> water to cover
> Bragg's to taste, diced
> 1 to 2 lemons, juiced

To Prepare

> Blend all ingredients well.

Health Benefits

- Provides fiber.

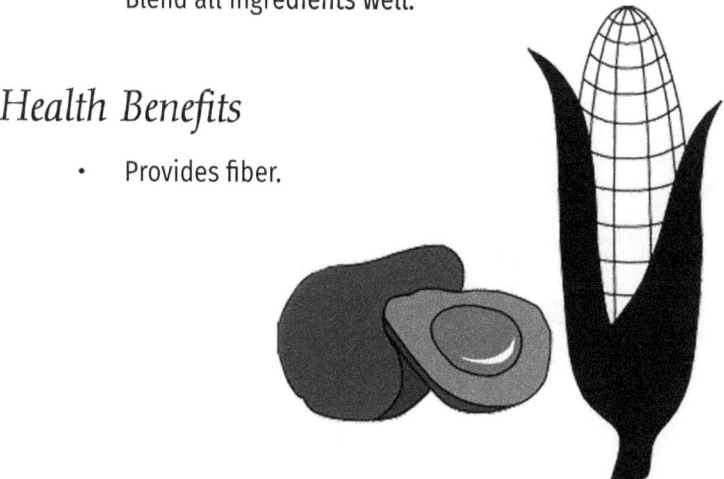

Mock Thousand Island Dressing

Ingredients

4 tomatoes
½ cup water
1 clove garlic, minced
1 small onion, quartered
1 Tbsp. dill weed
½ avocado or 1 Tbsp. of cold-pressed olive oil
1 Tbsp. Bragg's Aminos

To Prepare

Place all ingredients in a blender and blend until smooth.

Health Benefits

- High in vitamin C.

French-Style Salad Dressing

Ingredients

4 tomatoes
¼ cup lemon juice
4 Tbsp. cold-pressed olive oil
1 tsp. basil or oregano
2 cloves garlic or ¼ tsp. garlic powder

To Prepare

Wash tomatoes; remove stem and black spots. Cut up in quarter sections and place in blender. Blend all ingredients until smooth. Store in covered glass jar in refrigerator for 5 days. Makes two cups.

Health Benefits

- High in vitamin C.

Sesame-Garlic Dressing

Ingredients

⅓ blender of ground white sesame seeds (do not soak)
3 cloves garlic, sliced
½ blender of water or more if needed
1 tsp. turmeric
½ tsp. dill weed
Bragg's Aminos to taste
1 Tbsp. agave

For small serving:
1 cup white sesame seeds
2 cloves garlic
1 ¼ cup water
1 tsp. turmeric
½ tsp. dill
1 Tbsp. Braggs
1 Tbsp. agave

To Prepare

Blend well to smooth consistency. Should not be too stiff or too watery.

Health Benefits

- Provides calcium.
- Turmeric helps with digestion and assimilation. Also has antioxidant properties to control free radicals.

Live Green Goddess-Spanish

Ingredients

2 cups fresh spinach
1 stalk celery
2 cloves garlic, minced
2 cups water
1 avocado
1 lemon, juiced and seeded
1 Tbsp. Bragg's Aminos
1 tsp. thyme

To Prepare

Blend all ingredients except avocado. Add avocado last, for it will thicken mixture. Serve as an energy soup or salad dressing.

Health Benefits

- Provides chlorophyll and vitamin A.

Oil & Vinegar Dressing

Ingredients

- 3 cups cold-pressed extra virgin olive oil
- 5 garlic cloves, crushed
- 1 Tbsp. kelp
- ½ cup dry parsley
- 1 cup Bragg's raw apple cider vinegar
- 1 Tbsp. dry Italian seasoning (preferably organic)

To Prepare

Combine all ingredients in a bottle. Let marinate overnight. Can be used on everything.

Keeps indefinitely.

Health Benefits

- Helps to lubricate the body, build immune system and help with metabolism.

Mock Thousand Island Dressing #2

Ingredients

4-5 carrots water to cover
1 stalk celery
2-3 cloves garlic, sliced
1 lemon, juiced
1 avocado
½ tsp. celery seed
½ tsp. dill
½ tsp. parsley
½ tsp. thyme

To Prepare

Blend until smooth and serve. Can be used as an energy soup.

Health Benefits

- Contains beta carotene

Beet-Sunflower Seed Dressing

Ingredients

½ blender of beets, cut up
2 lemons, juiced
⅓ blender of sunflower seed sprouts
water to cover
Bragg's Aminos to taste

To Prepare

Blend all ingredients well.

Will keep 7 days in refrigerator.

Health Benefits

- Beets are powerful detoxifiers, and are good for cleansing the blood and liver.

Miso-Nayonaise Dressing

Ingredients

2 Tbsp. white organic miso
½ cup nayonaise
1 lemon, juiced
1 clove garlic, minced
¼ pure water

To Prepare

Mix miso and nayonaise until smooth, add lemon juice, garlic and water. Blend well.

Will keep seven days in refrigerator.

Health Benefits

- A low-fat dressing that is easy to prepare.
- The miso provides enzymes to help digest food.

Cranberry Sauce

Ingredients

1 lb. of cranberries, washed with stems removed
3 seedless sweet oranges
1 lemon, juiced (grate (zest) lemon before juicing)
zest from the lemon

To Prepare

Wash and remove stems from cranberries. Discard those that are spoiled. Pulse in food processor. Dice seedless oranges. Add to cranberries with lemon juice and lemon zest.

This is slightly tart; however, it complements the mock turkey and holiday dressing on pages 76 and 82.

Health Benefits

- Good to clean urinary tract.
- Should be used often when cranberries are in season.

Garlic Dressing

Ingredients

3 cups olive oil
5 cloves garlic, minced
1 Tbsp. kelp
½ cup dry parsley
1 tsp. dry Italian seasoning
1 Tbsp. Bragg's amino acids
½ cup lemon or lime juice

To Prepare

Mix all ingredients in a bottle.

Let marinate overnight. Delicious on all salads and steamed vegetables.

Health Benefits

- Garlic is known for its anti-bacterial action.
- Olive oil is the best oil to use for dressings, for it can be easily assimilated by the body.
- Use sparingly (high calorie)

Cucumber-Avocado Dressing

Ingredients

1 cucumber, cut in small pieces (peel if not organic)
1 stalk celery
½ medium onion
1 clove garlic, minced
1 Tbsp. Bragg's Aminos
1 Tbsp. dry Italian seasoning
½ avocado

To Prepare

Blend cucumber first; then all ingredients.

Health Benefits

- Cucumbers are good for the hair, nails and skin due to its silicon content.

Tomato Dressing

Ingredients

1 8-oz pkg. dehydrated tomatoes
2 cups water to hydrate tomatoes 3 hours
½ cup nutritional yeast
1 tsp. celtic sea salt
½ cup olive oil
2 tsp. Italian seasoning
2 garlic cloves
½ onion, minced
1 Tbsp. Braggs
3 tsp. maple syrup

To Prepare

Blend, add more water if necessary for consistency you prefer.

Health Benefits

The Supreme Machine!!

How much value would you put on a machine that is so special that there are no others like it, no spare parts and yet it must run continuously without stopping for up to 100 years — or more?

The machine, of course, is your body. The value assigned to it is up to you. But before you decide how much your body is worth, you should appreciate a few things about it. You ask it to do some phenomenal things, including process huge amounts of information, both input and output, on a daily basis; interface with others on many different levels, produce another human machine for continuity of the species, and, under certain circumstances, perform fetes of strength and courage.

Those things your body does because you tell it to; but what about all those things your body does every day, day after day, year after year, with little or no thought or decision on your part? Consider this for a moment — if you are an adult of about average weight, here's what you do in 24 hours:

- Your heart beats 108,689 times.
- Your hair grows .01714 inches.
- You breathe 23,040 times.
- You eat 3 pounds of food.
- You perspire 1.43 pints of liquid.
- You speak 4800 words.
- You turn 25 to 35 times in your sleep.
- You lose 7.8 pounds of waste weight.
- Your blood travels 168,000 miles.
- Your nails grow .000046 inches.
- You inhale 438 cubic feet of air.
- You drink 2.9 pounds of liquid.
- You move 750 major muscles.

It pays to take care of this fantastic, one-of-a-kind machine, since there are no spare parts!

Now that you have some idea of what this superb creation does, do you properly take care of it? It relentlessly performs its daily functions and asks only periodic attention, proper fuel, some rest, exercise, and an occasional checkup. Now that you know a little bit about what your body does and its minimum requirements, what is it worth? Of course, it is priceless, so be sure to maintain it with the basic requirements of proper nutrition, sleep and daily exercise.

— Source: *Vitality Labs Newsletter*

Desserts and Snacks

Various Snacks	79
Carrot Cake with Almond Icing	80
Sweet Potato Pie #1	81
Sweet Potato Pie #2	83
Apple Pie	85
Banana Cream Pudding	87
Banana Ice Cream	89
Victoria's Secret	90
Frankie's Cookies	91

The use of desserts is not encouraged. According to Dr. Nancy Appleton, author of *Lick the Sugar Habit*, sugar upsets the body chemistry, causing an imbalance in the body. The eating of sugar causes an increase in calcium and decreases the phosphorous in the blood, resulting in a deficiency in minerals, which hampers the enzymes' ability to digest food, causing food allergies.

Dr. Appleton believes that all simple sugars, including honey, fructose, maple syrup, malt, and rice syrup, interfere with the body's ability to digest food. It is estimated that the average person consumes 139 pounds of sugar annually. This is contributing to the increase in the incidence of diabetes in the American population. To explore this subject more, read *Lick the Sugar Habit*, by Nancy Appleton, Ph.D. You can order the book by calling 1-800-952-9665, or inquire about the book at your favorite book store.

Various Snacks

<u>Raisins and Sunflower Seeds</u>
>1 cup raisins (soaked)
>1 cup sprouted sunflower seeds
>
>Mix together to satisfy craving for sweets

<u>Oat, Raisins, Nuts</u>
>Combine equal portions of each

<u>Candied Sweets</u>
>Combine equal amounts of apricots, dates, coconut, nuts.

NOTE: These are hard on the digestive system, but better than simple sugar

<u>Nori Sheets</u>
>Eat one or two to satisfy craving for meats.

Health Benefits

<u>General benefits of snacks and desserts:</u>
- Nori sheets replace salt.
- Unsulphered apricots help with cancer.
- Dried fruit is better than sugar, but use sparingly, as it has lots of sugar itself.

Carrot Cake with Almond Icing

Ingredients

3 cups grated or ground carrots
1 cup soaked, chopped dried fruit
1 cup chopped walnuts or almonds
½ cup honey
tsp. cinnamon pinch of nutmeg wheat germ (optional)

Almond Frosting
2 cups ground almonds
1 tsp. honey
warm water

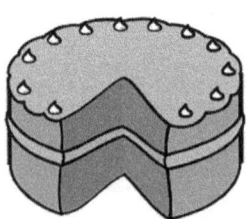

To Prepare

Run carrots through a Champion or grate fine. Add wheat germ if too moist to bind. Mix in other ingredients. Shape in form desired.

For frosting, add enough water to moisten almonds and whip with a fork. Add honey.

Sweet Potato Pie #1

(Using Champion with blank)

Ingredients

<u>Crust</u>
3/4 cup almonds (soaked)
3/4 cup sunflower seeds (soaked)
3 Tbsp. maple syrup
1 tsp. nutmeg
1 tsp. cinnamon

<u>Filling</u>
4 medium sweet potatoes, put through Champion with blank
1 cup pitted dates, soaked in ½ cup water
½ cup nuts (Brazil, pine, cashew) soaked
1 tsp. anise
1 tsp. cardamon
½ tsp. allspice

To Prepare

Make crust first. Grind soaked almonds and soaked sunflower seeds in Champion with blank. Add remaining ingredients and spread mixture in the bottom and around the sides of a 9- inch pie plate. Save ¼ of mixture to sprinkle on top.

Second, prepare filling by putting peeled potatoes through the Champion with the blank. Blend potatoes with dates, nuts and spices until smooth. Pour into pie crust and spread evenly.

Sprinkle remaining crust mixture around edge of pie. Refrigerate overnight before serving.

Pie will keep for 3 days in refrigerator

Health Benefits

- A raw pie has enzymes to help digest the pie. A cooked pie is devoid of enzymes.

Sweet Potato Pie #2

(Using Champion with blank)

Ingredients

Crust
1 cup ground flax
½ cup wheat germ

Filling
2 cups sweet potatoes
1 cup apples
1 Tbsp. psyllium
½ tsp. nutmeg
2 tsp. cinnamon
3 Tbsp. maple syrup
4 Tbsp. coconut (for decoration)
2 handsful of pine nuts
1 tsp. ginger
¼ cup raisins, soaked

To Prepare

Sprinkle ground flax into a 9-inch pie plate, covering bottom and sides of plate. Sprinkle wheat germ over flax. Puree sweet potatoes and apples in Champion with blank. Add remaining ingredients and pour mixture into the pie plate.

Decorate with coconut.

Health Benefits

- A raw pie has enzymes to help digest the pie. A cooked pie is devoid of enzymes.

Apple Pie

Ingredients

Filling
5 gala or golden delicious apples
1 cup soaked raisins
1 lemon, juiced
2 tsp. cinnamon
½ tsp. nutmeg
½ tsp. clove
½ cup golden flax, ground

Crust
12 dates
2 cups walnuts

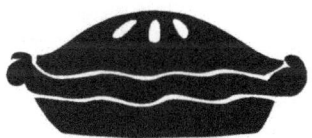

To Prepare

Filling: Wash apples and peel unless organic. Core apples. Place in food processor and pulse. Pour into a mixing bowl, add the lemon juice, coconut, cinnamon and nutmeg. Mix gently until lemon juice has covered all the apples. Add raisins, coconut powder, cinnamon and nutmeg.

<u>Prepare crust</u>: Process walnuts and dates in food processor with S blade until mixture comes together like a crust. Press into pie pan. Then pour apple mixture into crust mixture.

Sprinkle coconut or chopped walnuts on top. Refrigerate.

Can be served for breakfast.

Banana Cream Pudding

Ingredients

    1 cup ground flax seeds
    ½ cup raw wheat germ
    4 bananas
    1 lemon, juiced
    ½ cup coconut, shredded or flakes (not sugared, if possible)
    1 tsp. vanilla
    2 cups cashews
    1 cup apple cider or apple juice
    4 Tbsp. maple syrup

To Prepare

Cover bottom and sides of pie plate with ground flax seeds. Add wheat germ and gently pat out over the flax seeds.

In a separate bowl, slice bananas thinly, add lemon juice, maple syrup, coconut and vanilla, and gently mix. Pour mixture into the flax seed crust.

Blend 2 cups cashews with enough liquid (apple cider or apple juice or water to which 2 Tbsp. of maple syrup is added) to make a thick sauce. Start with one cup liquid, add more as needed a little at a time. Blend until smooth. Pour over banana mixture in pie plate. Decorate with coconut.

Note: Any fresh fruit can be substituted for bananas.

Health Benefits

- Desserts should be eaten only occasionally by a healthy person for it causes an imbalance in the body.
- Flax provides omega-3 and omega-6 essential fatty acids.

Banana Ice Cream

Ingredients

10 bananas
topping: chopped fruit, coconut, raisins, nuts, etc.

Ingredients

Freeze peeled bananas overnight in freezer bag. Put bananas through a Champion juicer with the blank. Put in serving dish and top with your favorite healthy topping.

Health Benefits

- Better than sugar-based ice cream.

Victoria's Secret

Ingredients

1 banana per person
2 cups frozen fruit
2 cups pure water
1 tsp. vanilla
1 avocado

To Prepare

Blend all ingredients until smooth. Pour in tall glasses.

Serve immediately.

Health Benefits

- Better than sugary drinks that are purchased at fast-food places.

Frankie's Cookies

Ingredients

1 quart soaked sunflower seeds
2 cups soaked almonds
2 cups soaked raisins
1 cup soaked dates
¼ cup coconut
1 cup soaked apricots
3-4 bananas
2 apples
1 cup coarse ground walnuts or pecans or whole raisins
½ tsp. cinnamon
½ tsp. vanilla

To Prepare

Put first 8 ingredients through Champion with blank. Save soak water from fruits for energy soup or to add to breakfast cereal as a sweetener. Discard soak water from nuts.

Add coarse nuts, whole raisins, cinnamon, and vanilla. Shape into cookies as you place on wax paper on dehydrator tray.

Turn once when firm. Keep refrigerated. Will keep for 30 days.

Health Benefits

- Use occasionally to satisfy desire for sweets.

Balancing Live Foods

Daily schedule for meeting nutritional requirements

- Eat six cups of a variety of sprouts and vegetables daily, either in soups, as juice, or in recipes. Make sure you eat a minimum of one cup of sprouts.
- Eat two large salads every day using a variety of sprouts, vegetables and greens, served with a vegetable-, seed- or avocado-based dressing.
- Drink two eight-ounce glasses of fresh juice — vegetable or fruit — daily.
- Eat two types of fresh fruit daily, preferably for breakfast.
- Use three to eight ounces of seed cheese or yogurt made from sprouts and fermented seeds or nuts each day. If you want to gain weight, eat six to eight ounces; if you want to lose weight, eat three ounces.
- Three or four times a week, use avocado, raw honey, sprouted or soaked nuts and soaked dried fruit for added calories.
- Use at least one to three ounces of fresh wheatgrass juice daily for two weeks and then use same amount once or twice per week. Sip slowly and take on an empty stomach. If you cannot tolerate it orally, take a rectal implant daily.
- Eat as much of properly combined meals as to satisfy your hunger. Eat more food if you are having trouble maintaining your ideal weight, which should be 15 to 20 pounds less than the so-called average. The extra weight on Americans is due to the heavy emphasis on animal fat.
- Use seaweeds daily in energy soup or salads.

Note: In reference to alfalfa sprouts, according to Dr. Andrew Weil, alfalfa sprouts contain canavanine, a toxin that can harm the immune system. Therefore, individuals who are chronically ill should refrain from using alfalfa sprouts and other legumes and use non- leguminous sprouts, such as sunflower, broccoli, radish, buckwheat, etc.

Basics

Make sure that you chew your food thoroughly when you eat. It is most beneficial to eat in small amounts more frequently throughout the day. However, here are some suggestions for the usual mealtimes:

Breakfast — At breakfast, smoothies are ideal. Simple combinations of fruits (apple and avocado) are excellent. A nice combination is apple and banana. Watermelon juice is another good treat in the morning. Sprouted buckwheat cereal is a favorite of all the students at the Ann Wigmore Institute in Puerto Rico. If used sparingly, milks such as sesame can be used for breakfast. Greens and apples blended with rejuvelac makes for a satisfying and cleansing treat.

Lunch — Of course, energy soup is the main dish. Vege-kraut, almond Crème or a few dehydrated foods can be had if you're really hungry.

Dinner — Again, energy soup is the main dish. Avoid eating too late at night.

Occasionally, have a few grain crisps or protein nuggets as a special snack. These are only for occasional variety and should be used sparingly.

Proteins

Mock Turkey	*96*
Seed Cheese	*97*
Almond Crème	*98*
Sesame Milk	*99*
Almond Cabbage Loaf	*100*
Sunflower Seed Loaf	*101*
Holiday Dressing	*102*
Sunflower-Sesame Seed Cheese	*103*
Nancy's Almond Loaf	*105*

Mock Turkey

Ingredients

- 1 small bunch of celery (put through Champion with blank
- 1 cup green onions, chopped
- 2 sprigs parsley, minced
- 1 cup almonds or pecans, soaked and put through Champion
- 1 avocado, mashed
- 1 tsp. ground sage
- 1 lemon, juiced and seeded
- 1 Tbsp. Bragg's Aminos

To Prepare

Wash all vegetables. Put celery and nuts through the Champion with blank. Add finely chopped onions, minced parsley, mashed avocado and ground sage, juice of one lemon and 1 Tbsp. of Bragg's. Mix all ingredients. Shape in a loaf. If creative, shape as a turkey.

Serve on bed of romaine lettuce with Cranberry Sauce and Holiday Dressing.

Health Benefits

- Substitute for meat.
- Proper combination of vegetables and protein (nuts and avocado).

Seed Cheese

Ingredients

1 cup sunflower seeds, soaked overnight
1 cup almonds, soaked overnight or 8 hours
1 cup sesame seeds, soaked overnight
1 cup pumpkin seeds, soaked overnight
2 lemons, juiced and seeded
1 onion, diced
1 red pepper, diced
3 cloves garlic, minced
¼ cup dry parsley
3 Tbsp. dry Italian seasoning paprika

To Prepare

Blend all soaked nuts and seeds together with 4 cups or more of water until smooth. Pour into a bag or cotton towel and let drip for 12 hours. Add remaining ingredients. Shape in a loaf or serve in a glass bowl. Sprinkle with paprika.

Health Benefits

- Source of protein. Also contains calcium and zinc.

Almond Crème

Ingredients

2 cups almonds, soaked overnight or 8 hours
2 cups or more water to make a cream
1 lemon, juiced
2 Tbsp. maple syrup

To Prepare

Soak almonds overnight or at least 8 hours. Drain and add enough boiling water to cover nuts. Let set one minute. Pour off hot water and de-hull almonds. This is time-consuming, so get someone to help.

Health Benefits

- Almonds help to alkalize the body. They should be used more frequently than any other nut.
- A good source of protein.

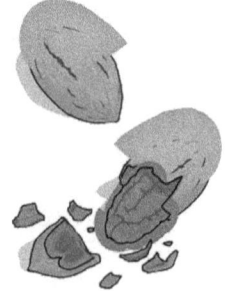

Sesame Milk

Ingredients

2 cups white sesame seeds, ground
4 cups water
1 lemon, juiced and seeded
3 Tbsp. maple syrup
1 tsp. vanilla

To Prepare

Grind sesame seeds in a coffee grinder. Place in blender, add 2 cups of water, and blend until the milk flows, approximately 3 minutes. Add remaining water and blend on low speed.

Add maple syrup, lemon juice and vanilla. Blend 15 seconds. Strain and store milk in glass container. Discard sesame pulp, for it is difficult to digest.

Will keep 3 days.

Health Benefits

- Supplies needed calcium for building strong bones. Also very good for people who want to gain weight.

Almond Cabbage Loaf

Ingredients

1 medium green cabbage, cut in pieces to go through Champion
3 cups almonds, soaked overnight or 12 hours
1 large sweet onion
2 cloves garlic
½ cup of fresh lemon juice
2 Tbsp. of Bragg's Aminos
2 Tbsp. of dill weed
1 avocado, mashed

To Prepare

Put the first four ingredients through Champion with blank. Add lemon juice, Bragg's and dill weed and mashed avocado. Mix thoroughly. Shape into a loaf. Decorate with sprouts or vegetables. Refrigerate for two hours before serving.

Health Benefits

- Provides protein.

Sunflower Seed Loaf

Ingredients

½ cups soaked sunflower seeds
2 medium carrots
2 cloves garlic, minced
1 medium onion, quartered
¼ cup sweet basil
1 lemon, juiced and seeded

To Prepare

Put the first four ingredients listed through Champion with blank. Add remaining ingredients. Mix well. Shape into loaf. Serve on romaine lettuce leaves or surround with sprouts or tomatoes.

Health Benefits

- Source of protein.

Holiday Dressing

Ingredients

4 cups soaked sunflower seeds
1 cup pumpkin seeds, soaked
1 tsp. sage
½ cup chopped celery
¼ cup chopped onion
1 clove garlic, minced
½ lemon, juiced
2-3 tsp. Bragg's Aminos

To Prepare

Blend sunflower seeds and pumpkin seeds with enough water (5 cups or more) until smooth. Place in bags or in dish towel and let water drip out. Let set 12 hours to ferment.

Add remaining ingredients. Mix thoroughly.

Best when made a day before it is to be used to let flavors blend.

Health Benefits

- Source of protein to be served with vegetables for proper food combining.

Sunflower-Sesame Seed Cheese

Ingredients

1 cup white sesame seeds
4 cups distilled water
(above ingredients for sesame milk)

1 ½ cups sesame milk
2 cups sprouted sunflower seeds (sprouted one day)
1 tsp. cumin
1 tsp. dill weed 1 tsp. dulse
2 cloves garlic
1 lemon, juiced

To Prepare

Prepare sesame milk first. Place 1 cup of sesame seeds in blender, add 2 cups water, blend until the milk flows. Add remaining water, blend 2 minutes. Then strain (divide milk from pulp). Store milk in glass jar. Save seeds for cookies.

Combine 1 ½ cups sesame milk and remaining ingredients. Blend and put in a jar with a lid. Ferment for 4-8 hours.

Health Benefits

- Provides protein and calcium. This is a tasty seed cheese recipe.

Nancy's Almond Loaf

Ingredients

1 quart soaked almonds
3 large carrots
4 stalks celery
¾ cup green pepper or red pepper
1 medium sweet onion
3 cloves garlic
2 lemons, juiced
1 Tbsp. Bragg's Aminos

To Prepare

Use blank in Champion juicer. Alternate almonds and vegetables to avoid damage to motor. End with celery and then carrots to push nuts through. Mix by hand in large bowl. Add lemon juice, then Bragg's. Will keep in refrigerator up to 7 days.

Health Benefits

- Protein.

Most Dangerous Foods

1. **WHITE SUGAR** — Robs the body of vitamins, especially vitamin E.

   Causes drowsiness, temper, violence. Damages soft tissues of the heart, kidneys, and liver.

   Substituting with artificial sweeteners is dangerous. Kills the immune system (vital to fight disease).

   Sweeteners should be used sparingly.

2. **WHITE FLOUR** — Causes constipation, increases sugar level.

   ABSOLUTELY NO NUTRIENTS!

3. **SOFT DRINKS** — Kidney problems, weakness, and loss of eyesight.

   Draws phosphorous out of bones. Possible cause of osteoporosis.

4. **RED MEAT** — Bacteria infested. Cancer causing. Increases *the* workload of the kidneys and liver. Inflammation of the nerves and muscles. Often worm infested.

5. **COFFEE & TEA** — Caffeine dramatically devastates the nervous system.

6. **DAIRY PRODUCTS** — (Ice cream, cheese, yogurt) Dangerous chemicals injected, mucous forming, inability to digest (especially in blacks).

   ALTERNATIVES: Safflower butter, soy cheese, rice dream, rice, soy milk, sesame milk, almond Crème.

7. **TAP WATER** — Full of foreign matter. Active viruses, bacteria, and chemicals that cause cancer, kidney stones, constipation, arthritis, inflamed intestinal tract. Excessively high chlorine content.

8. **ALCOHOL** — Robs the body of nutrients, over-works the kidneys. Often leads to cirrhosis of the liver and mental disability.

Dehydrated Foods

Dehydration Class 108
    Dehydrated Bananas 108
    Protein Nuggets 109
    Bread Replacements 109
    Basic Bread 109
    Grain Crisps 110

Recipes
    George's Crackers – Papadam Style 111
    Everybody's Favorite Crackers 112
    Garden Burgers 113
    Banana-Nut Pancakes 115

Dehydration Class

Dehydrating became very popular because people like snacks and were not choosing the healthiest snacks. People were also using a lot of dried fruit from stores. As a result, too many people were experiencing stomach aches. You can make your own dehydrated snacks using leftovers, especially bananas and seed cheese and any kind of nut.

Food dehydration is a process of slowly heating foods at a low temperature so as to not destroy nutrients. Food dehydrators usually have temperature settings. Do not set your dehydrator over 110-115 degrees because temperatures higher than these will destroy enzymes. Food dehydrators come in various sizes. Dehydrated foods, when carried with you when you do your shopping or traveling or whatever else, will assist you in overcoming any addictions you may have to unhealthy snacks.

Dehydrated foods are not recommended as a main course food. Energy soups are the most important food. **Dehydrated foods are for occasional snacks and celebrations.**

General Instructions

Dehydrated Bananas

Bananas are generally sweeter and fuller in nutrients as they mature. Use those that are speckled and dark, but with the insides still perfect. Peel the bananas. Cut them in half. Then cut each half the long way, making four pieces. Thin banana chips do not seem to work as well as these strips. The cut side should lie flat on the sheet. The bananas will need to be turned so the other side will dry. They should not dry until they are excessively hard. A few days should be sufficient drying time.

Protein Nuggets

Protein nuggets are similar to a tasty cookie and are generally loved by everybody. Soak hulled (shell removed) sunflower seeds and add enough rejuvelac to cover. Blend. Add bananas and keep adding them until the blender is full. If necessary, add more rejuvelac. Pour the batter on the dehydrator sheets in the size of cookies. After a few days, turn them over if they are ready. Some people like them chewy, and some people like them harder and crisper. You decide! Excellent for traveling!

Bread Replacements

All different types of crackers and breads can be made with a dehydrator. Add certain seasonings and you can have pizza. You can even make a type of banana cracker. Use your imagination to create all kinds of tasty treats.

Basic Bread

This is the basic recipe for bread. Use your imagination for variations. Soak soft pastry wheat (or any grain) for 8 to 10 hours. Sprout the grain for about two days. Fill the blender about one-half full with grain sprouts. Add enough rejuvelac to make a "pancake like" batter (for variations add a few bananas, dates or vegetables etc.) Pour onto dehydrator sheets. Bread usually dehydrates faster than other dehydrated foods.

One of the greatest advantages of dehydrated foods is that nothing ever has to be thrown away. Dehydrate seed cheese, almond crème, smoothies, cereals and any other leftovers. Even energy soup can be dehydrated. If you like, blend in a few bananas before you dehydrate energy soup to make a nice soup cracker. Vege-kraut and seed cheese mixed together is a nice treat.

Grain Crisps

Variety of nourishment and the need for concentrated and valuable nutrients to take care of the immediate needs of unhealthy people is important. Grain crisps help furnish these needed nutrients. It is not advisable for cancer victims to eat such concentrated food.

Grain crisps are very simple to make. Grains used can be rice, millet, barley, oats, rye, and/or wheat. With the exception of rice, all are soaked for twelve hours; rice is soaked for twenty-four hours. Next, the grain should be sprouted another twelve hours. The sprouted grain is then blended in a Vita-Mix with rejuvelac to a very thin, paste-like consistency that is easily spread — generally one cup of grain to one cup of rejuvelac.

As you blend, different flavors can be added. For a banana/grain crisp, you would use two bananas to one cup of grain and one cup of rejuvelac. Banana and carrots can be used together. For cinnamon grain crisp, add about two tablespoons of cinnamon to your paste. If you want a sweeter flavor, add an herb mixture, and for a vegetable grain crisp, you can add onions or any desired vegetable. Sea vegetables can also be used: dulse, kelp or Irish moss, and they will

provide needed minerals, as well as vitamins E, D, and A, and calcium and magnesium. Place mixture in dehydrator until crisp. (115/ for approximately one to two days.)

Source: Ann Wigmore, D.D., Ph.D., N.D.

George's Crackers – Papadam Style

Ingredients

2 cups flax seeds, soaked
2 cups almonds (soaked)
2 cups sunflower seeds (soaked)
4 Tbsp. Bragg's Aminos
1 onion
cayenne pepper
caraway seeds
parsley
dill weed garlic
or anything your heart desires

To Prepare

Blend and dehydrate very thin.

Everybody's Favorite Crackers

Ingredients

1 cup soaked sunflower seeds
1 cup soaked walnuts
1 cup soaked almonds
1 tomato
1 cup red onion, chopped
3 Tbsp. flaxseed
3 tsp. cumin seed
2 tsp. salt

To Prepare

Mix in food processor or Champion juicer with blank on. Spread on parchment paper or Teflon sheets. Make them very thin. Using a pizza cutter, cut in squares. They will be easier to break into pieces when dry. Dehydration time is about 15- 20 hours.

Garden Burgers

Ingredients

3 Tbsp. flax seeds, ground
6 Tbsp. water
1 cup carrot pulp
1 cup sunflower seeds, ground
½ cup finely minced celery
6 Tbsp. finely minced onion
2 Tbsp. finely minced parsley
2 Tbsp. finely minced red pepper
2 tsp Bragg's Aminos

To Prepare

In a blender, combine the ground flax seeds and water; blend thoroughly. Immediately pour the mixture into a bowl and set aside. (Rinse the blender container immediately before the mixture left in it hardens and becomes difficult to wash out.)

In a medium-sized bowl, thoroughly mix the carrot pulp, sunflower seeds, celery, onion, parsley, red pepper and liquid aminos. Add the flax seed mixture and mix thoroughly. Add more water if necessary so that the mixture can be formed into patties. Form into six ½ inch (1 cm) thick patties. Place immediately in the dehydrator and dehydrate the burgers for 4 to 8 hours, leave them in the sun until warm or place them in a warm oven for 10 to 15 minutes.

Makes 6 patties.

Banana-Nut Pancakes

Ingredients

½ cups barley, soaked 3 days
½ cup purified water or apple juice
1 banana
1 Tbsp. raw honey
½ cup raw soaked, chopped pecans
1-2 tsp. cinnamon
1 tsp. vanilla

To Prepare

Soak barley for three days, rinsing night and morning, until grains are soft in the center. (Squeeze one in fingers to see if there is a hard center.)

In blender, mix barley with ¼ cup liquid (enough to cover). Add banana and spices. Add additional liquid, blending until fairly smooth, forming a dough that is thicker than pancake batter, but will still move in the blender. Add chopped soaked nuts, and gently stir in. If the dough needs to be thicker, add additional nuts.

Fill ¼ cup measure with "dough." Turn on to a teflex sheet, and spread to form uniform ½» thick circles. Dehydrate at 110 degrees for 2 hours. Remove from teflex sheet, and turn over onto mesh screen. Dehydrate for additional 2 hours. (The smaller you make them, the less time it takes to dehydrate.) Serve warm or store dried "bread" in zip lock bags in freezer or refrigerator. Will keep for several weeks if sealed.

Makes 6 to 8. Five minutes to prepare.

Five Basic Rules of Food Combining

1. Liquids alone
2. Dense carbohydrates
   or
   Dense proteins with leafy greens and vegetables
3. Fruits alone
4. Acid fruits
   or
   Sweet fruits with subacid fruits
5. Melons alone

Miscellaneous Recipes

Gwen's Pizza 120

Noor's Recipes 123

Breakfast Tart With Banana Sauce 124

Tabouli 126

Squash Royale Energy Soup 127

Hiawatha's & Lou's Barley Bread and Sandwich Spread 128

Fig & Papaya Anti Aging Salad 129

Hiawatha's Awesome Sesame Garlic Dressing 132

Hiawatha's Cabbage Salad 133

Yummy Italian Dressing 134

Apple Pie 135

Lasagna – Victoria's Recipe 136

Caroline's Supreme Sunflower Seed Paté 138

Jade's Seed Cheese (non-fermented) 139

Jade's Fabulous Hummus 140

Raw Cream of Broccoli Soup 141

Nori Rolls 142

Arame Cabbage Marinade 144

Avocado Dressing 145

Maxine's Natural French Dressing *146*
Oatmeal *147*
Cashew Crème *148*
Almond Crème *149*
Cleopatra Carrot Cake *150*
Queen Elinor Cream Frosting *151*
Banana/Coconut/Tahini Cream Pie* *152*
Cranberry Salad *154*
Mother Knows Best Salad *155*
Jade's Sensuous Salmon *156*
Sweet Onion Relish *157*

Try these optional seasonings to taste:

- Italian seasoning from Frontier
- celery leaf from Frontier
- veggie broth from Frontier
- Bragg's Aminos
- parsley
- dill
- cayenne
- oregano
- basil
- splash of apple cider vinegar and olive oil

Gwen's Pizza

Ingredients

Crust

2 ½ cups buckwheat groats, soaked 6 hours, sprouted 24 hours

⅓ cup extra-virgin olive oil

3-4 Tbsp. herbs or spices, or more to taste:
- a. dried basil
- b. oregano
- c. dried red chili peppers
- d. sea salt

liquid aminos

To Prepare

Put in processor until a dough is formed. Shape into crust approximately one-fourth inch thick and put in dehydrator. Let get hard and dry all the way through.

Pizza "Cheese"

Start 8-12 hours ahead of assembly time:

2 cups of soaked cashews

1 Tbsp. lemon juice rejuvelac (see page 127)

2-4 Tbsp. raw tahini

raw miso, light or dark 2 cloves garlic, pressed
red cayenne pepper (optional)

To Prepare

Mix both together in Vita-Mix with enough rejuvelac to make a fairly thin paste. Place in a bowl and cover with a cloth; let it sit 8-12 hours in a dark place in order to ferment (not in refrigerator). After fermentation, add raw tahini. Mix by hand. Add miso, garlic and red pepper. Do not refrigerate.

Ingredients

Pizza Sauce

1 cup fresh tomatoes, chopped
¼ cup onion, chopped
½ cup sun-dried tomatoes, chopped
½ tsp. garlic, minced
⅓ tsp. jalapeno, minced 4 fresh basil leaves
½ cup medjool dates, pitted
olive oil or fresh tomato juice for blending
¼ cup Bragg's Aminos or 1 teaspoon Celtic sea salt
⅛ cup maple syrup
1 Tbsp. olive oil

To Prepare

Combine the above ingredients in a food processor or a blending jar and blend. Add a little tomato juice or olive oil if the sauce is too thick to blend. Stir in Bragg's or Celtic sea salt, maple syrup and olive oil. Keeps for two days in the refrigerator. Makes 2 ½ cups.

Pizza Veggies

(Chop veggies fine)
½ cup red pepper

½ cup olives
½ cup onions 1 cup zucchini
2 cups sliced porta bella mushrooms

Assembly

Layer in this order:

1. Cheese
2. Sauce
3. Veggies
4. Mushrooms

Sprinkle ground fenugreek if desired

Noor's Recipes

Hummus
⅓ gallon jar of sprouted chickpeas
1 ½ lemon, juiced
¼ cup olive oil
4 cloves garlic
1 onion
¼ to ½ cup of soaked sesame seeds
¼ to ½ tsp. Celtic salt
pepper, thyme, basil, ginger to taste

Blend until thick and creamy

Noor's Famous Salad Dressing
½ cup soaked sesame seeds, with water
1 cup soaked sunflower seeds, with water
1 to 1 ½ lemon, juiced
1 tsp. thyme
1 tsp. basil
¼ tsp. Celtic salt
¼ tsp. black pepper or chili pepper
3 cloves garlic
½ onion
2 cups olive oil

Tahini
1 pound brown sesame seeds, not soaked
½ cup oil (sesame preferably)
Blend well

Breakfast Tart With Banana Sauce

Ingredients

Crust:

1 cup almonds soaked 12-48 hours and blanched
1 cup sunflower seeds, soaked 6-8 hours
½ cup mission figs
1 teaspoon cinnamon

Filling:

2 apples, shredded in food processor
3 tsp. psyllium
1 tsp. vanilla
1 tsp. cinnamon

To Prepare

Process crust ingredients in Champion with blank and press into pie pan. Combine filling ingredients and pour into crust. Frost with Lou's Banana Sauce

Lou's Banana Sauce

For Breakfast Tart

Ingredients

3 bananas
½ cup coconut
½ cup water

To Prepare

Blend until smooth.

Tabouli

Ingredients

1 cup kamut (soaked)
2 bunches parsley
1 red pepper
1 small onion
1 Tbsp. olive oil
1 lemon, juiced
basil, thyme and sea salt to taste

To Prepare

Combine all ingredients.

Squash Royale Energy Soup

Ingredients

- 2 cups butternut squash
- 2 oranges
- 2 tangerines
- 2 cups rejuvelac
- 2 cups celery
- ½ tsp. cardamon
- ½ tsp. cinnamon
- ½ tsp. nutmeg

To Prepare

Blend all ingredients. Serves six.

Hiawatha's & Lou's Barley Bread and Sandwich Spread

Ingredients

Bread

4 cups barley, soaked and processed through Champion
4 Tbsp. olive oil
1 cup soaked oats or
½ cup flax seed, ground
1 cup millet
1 tsp. sea salt
2 Tbsp. Salad Supreme or a mixture of your favorite herbs — thyme, basil, etc.

Sandwich Spread

1 avocado
½ lemon, juiced
½ tsp. dill weed
2 Tbsp. rejuvelac

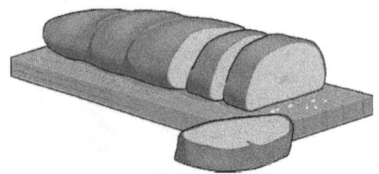

To Prepare

Combine bread ingredients, shape into a loaf and dehydrate 12 hours; turn and dehydrate 6 hours.

Combine sandwich spread ingredients and spread on sliced bread. Serve immediately.

Fig & Papaya Anti Aging Salad

Ingredients

Salad

12 fresh, ripe Calimyrna figs or soaked black mission figs, cut into wedges.

2 papayas, peeled, seeded and sliced (fresh mangoes can be used)

⅓ head napa cabbage, cut into 2-inch chunks

1 red bell pepper, julienned

1 cup red currant tomatoes or small cherry or grape tomatoes

1 orange or tangerine, peeled and sliced.

Dressing

3 Tbsp. honey

¼ cup rice vinegar

¼ cup olive oil

1 Tbsp. black sesame seeds

1 tsp. salt

½ tsp pepper

To Prepare

Combine ingredients of salad except for orange or tangerine. Combine ingredients of dressing and whisk until well blended. When ready to serve, mix dressing with salad. Garnish with orange or tangerine slices.

Garlic Dressing

Ingredients

6 cloves garlic, minced 1 cup nutritional yeast
1 cup olive oil
1 cup water
2 lemons, juiced
½ tsp. Celtic salt

To Prepare

Blend together.

Hiawatha's Awesome Sesame Garlic Dressing

Ingredients

½ cup unhulled sesame seeds
1 ½ cups water
3-5 cloves garlic
1 tsp. dill weed
1 tsp. turmeric
½ tsp. Celtic salt or Bragg's Aminos

To Prepare

Grind sesame seeds in coffee grinder. Put all ingredients in Vita-Mix and blend.

Hiawatha's Cabbage Salad

Ingredients

1 small head green cabbage, shredded
¼ red pepper, diced
2 stalks celery, chopped fine but not minced
2 medium onions, minced
2 carrots, grated
Add the following to taste:
- fennel seed
- ginger
- dry mustard
- Bragg's Aminos

To Prepare

Combine all ingredients in a bowl.

Yummy Italian Dressing

Ingredients

2 lemons, juiced
1 cup extra virgin olive oil
2 Tbsp. flax seeds
1 tsp. oregano
1 tsp. Italian herbs mix
1 Tbsp. fennel seeds
1 bulb garlic
1 onion
1 Tbsp. apple cider vinegar
1 Tbsp. honey
1 tsp. cayenne pepper
½ tsp. sea salt

To Prepare

Blend all ingredients together in a bowl and let set at least four hours before serving.

Apple Pie

(From the Ann Wigmore Institute, Puerto Rico)

Ingredients

Crust

2 cups wheat, sprouted 24 hours
1 cup sunflower seeds, soaked 5-6 hours
   or
2 cups walnuts
6 pitted dates

Filling

½ cup soaked raisins
½ cup soaked dates
10 large or 15 small apples cinnamon to taste

To Prepare

Put crust ingredients through Champion with blank two times. For sweeter crust, add some raisins or dates. Spread over bottom of pie dish or platter.

Blend raisins and/or dates with soak water until thick. Add a dash of cinnamon. Peel and slice apples into very thin slices. On crust, layer with sliced apples and raisin/date mixture alternatively. Top with some raisins. Refrigerate or chill for at least a couple hours before serving.

Lasagna – Victoria's Recipe

Ingredients & Preparation

Cheese (Start 8-12 hours ahead of assembly time)

2 cups cashews, soaked
1 Tbsp. lemon juice rejuvelac (see page 127)
2-4 Tbsp. raw tahini
2 Tbsp. miso, raw light or dark
2 cloves garlic, pressed
red pepper (optional)

Blend cashews and lemon juice together with enough rejuvelac to make a fairly thin paste. Place in a bowl and cover with a cloth; let sit 8-12 hours in a dark place in order to ferment (not in refrigerator). After fermentation, add raw tahini and mix by hand; add miso, garlic and red pepper. Do not refrigerate.

Red Sauce (Start 2-3 hours ahead of assembly time)

4-6 dates, soaked 2-3 hours; do not pour the water off
2 cloves garlic
2 heaping Tbsp. soaked basil or ¾ cup of fresh basil
2 cups sun-dried tomatoes

Combine and cover with water and soak, adding water to keep ingredients covered until soft. Then blend.

Marinate
¾ tsp. each of thyme, oregano and basil
¼ tsp. ground mustard (grind in a coffee grinder)
¼ tsp. Celtic salt
c tsp. cayenne or black pepper or ground up red peppers for really hot
¼-½ cup olive oil
¼-½ Tbsp. lemon juice commensurate with olive oil

Refrigerate to marinate

Body (Start from 2 hours to a day ahead of time)
3-4 medium sized zucchini, sliced very thin (use Saladacco or carrot peeler)
1 pound spinach, leaves only

Pour marinate over zucchini and let sit from 2 hours to all day. Drain in colander. Use the drippings from the colander filled with the zucchini to coat spinach leaves.

Assembly
Layer one-half of the zucchini on the bottom of 9" x 13" pan. Spread the cheese on top of the zucchini. Cut up enough Portobello or other large mushrooms to form the next layer. Layer on the rest of the zucchini. Pour on one-half of the red sauce. Layer on the spinach which was marinated in the zucchini drippings. Pour on the rest of the red sauce over the top, using a spatula. Top with remainder of the mushrooms and some black olives for decoration.

Caroline's Supreme Sunflower Seed Paté

Ingredients

4 cups sprouted sunflower seeds
1 cup soaked almonds or sprouted pumpkin seeds
6-8 medium carrots
1 medium onion, chopped fine
2 stalks celery, chopped fine
¼ cup parsley, minced
1 tsp. curry powder
4 cloves garlic, minced or crushed
2 lemons, juiced
2 avocados, mashed
See optional seasonings, page 100

To Prepare

Grind first three ingredients through Champion juicer with the blank (carrots can be juiced for a dryer consistency). Mix well with rest of ingredients; form into a loaf, decorate and serve.

Jade's Seed Cheese (non-fermented)

Ingredients

10 cups soaked sunflower seeds
8 cloves garlic
2 bunches celery, diced
2-3 red onions, diced
8 cloves garlic, diced
1 cup lemon juice
1 bunch parsley, minced
Bragg's Aminos, olive oil and apple cider vinegar to taste
See optional seasonings, page 100. Also chili powder, dulse, kelp powder and cayenne pepper

To Prepare

Put garlic and sunflower seeds through Champion with the blank; add rest of ingredients and mix.

Jade's Fabulous Hummus

Ingredients

4 cups chickpeas/garbanzo beans, sprouted
5 cloves garlic
2 avocados
2-3 lemons, juiced
1 bunch broccoli
1-2 red onions or to taste
2-3 red bell peppers
1 package celery
2 yellow bell peppers
Optional: add any pretty vegetable
See optional seasonings, page 100

To Prepare

Blend first four ingredients with water in Vita-Mix

Dice and add the rest of the ingredients and season to taste.

Raw Cream of Broccoli Soup

Ingredients

½ cup coconut, unsweetened
1 cup raw cashews, soaked for 2 hours or
1 cup sunflower seeds, soaked for 2 hours (or mix the two)
½ cup olive oil
3 cloves garlic
3 stalks celery
½ jalapeno pepper sea salt to taste
½ tsp. raw honey
1 tomato (optional)
2 large stalks broccoli

To Prepare

Put all ingredients except broccoli in blender or food processor and add water, approximately one-half full. Add more water to make the mixture the consistency of pancake batter. Add peeled broccoli stems. Blend at high speed. Add flowerettes at low speed so there will be some chunks in the soup.

Nori Rolls

Ingredients

Nori sheets
2 cups pumpkin seeds, soaked one hour (make pumpkin seed paté)
8 cloves garlic
1 large onion
Bragg's Aminos or Shoya to taste

Quantities of the following depend on the number of rolls you make and the ingredients you like the most.

red bell pepper
yellow bell pepper
red onion
romaine lettuce
cucumber
avocados
scallions – one for each roll

Dip
Amount needed depends on number of nori rolls

Bragg's Aminos
olive oil
scallions
chili powder

To Prepare

Combine pumpkin seeds, garlic, onion and Bragg's or Shoya with water to cover and blend in Vita-Mix. Put in bag or strainer and let set for six hours.

Lay a nori sheet flat and spread with the pumpkin seed paté. Layer the nori sheets down the middle with the vegetables cut into thin, long strips. Roll up the sheet. Using a sharp knife, cut in half.

Mix ingredients for dip in blender and mix well and often.

Arame Cabbage Marinade

Ingredients

½ head white cabbage
½ head purple cabbage rejuvelac (see page 127)
2 cups arame, soaked 5 minutes
1 onion, diced
2-3 carrots, grated
2-3 lemons, juiced

To Prepare

Chop cabbage to the consistency of coleslaw and cover with rejuvelac. Combine with remaining ingredients and mix thoroughly.

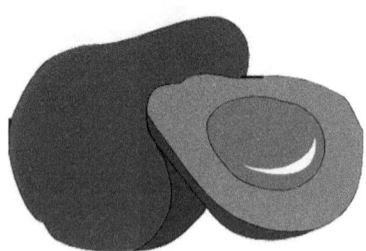

Avocado Dressing

Ingredients

avocados
4 cloves garlic
½ to 1 red onion
splash of apple cider vinegar and olive oil
Bragg's Aminos or Shoya to taste
seasoning to taste

To Prepare

Combine all ingredients in Vita-Mix, cover with water and blend thoroughly.

For Red Bell Pepper Dressing, add 2-3 red bell peppers.

Maxine's Natural French Dressing

Ingredients

3 pounds fresh or frozen tomatoes
¼ cup olive oil
A few drops of stevia to taste
1 small onion
1 clove garlic
1 tsp. sweet basil
3 lemons, juiced
1 Tbsp. kelp, onion powder or garlic powder

To Prepare

Blend in Vita-Mix. Add water to desired thickness. If using fresh tomatoes, adjust water as necessary.

Oatmeal

Ingredients

2 cups oat groats, soaked 2 days (change water 2 times daily)
2 cups rejuvelac (see page 127)
cinnamon and vanilla to taste

To Prepare

Blend well. Add one more cup of rejuvelac (optional) and blend well again.

Serve with any or all of the following:

rehydrated raisins or apricots
pine nuts
raw honey
sesame milk
almond milk

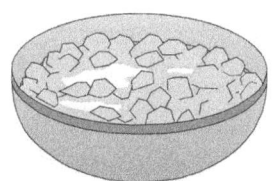

Sesame Milk — Grind 1 cup hulled sesame seeds in coffee grinder and blend well with 2 ½ cups water

Almond Milk — add 8 ounces of water to 2 tablespoons of almond crème.

Cashew Crème

Ingredients

1 cup cashews, soaked 1 hour in water or apple juice to cover

2 Tbsp. maple syrup (omit if apple juice is used)

1 tsp. vanilla

nutmeg, cardamon or cinnamon (optional)

To Prepare

Blend all ingredients in Vita-Mix

Almond Crème

Ingredients

1 cup almonds, soaked for 12 hours
2 Tbsp. maple syrup
1 tsp. vanilla
nutmeg, cardamon or cinnamon (optional)

To Prepare

Drain soaked almonds, cover with boiling water and let set approximately three minutes; then remove skins.

Blend all ingredients in Vita-Mix with water to cover.

Cleopatra Carrot Cake

Ingredients

1 cup black mission figs, soaked 1 hour in ½ cup water
⅔ cup raisins, soaked 1 hour in ½ cup water
⅓ cup pitted dates, soaked 1 hour in ¼ cup water
⅔ cup pine nuts
1 cup walnut pieces
4 cups finely grated carrots (about 6 large carrots)
1 cup shredded, unsweetened coconut
½ tsp. ground ginger
½ tsp. ground cloves

To Prepare

Drain soaked fruit and, if desired, save water (can be saved for six weeks) for use in recipes that call for soak water or for use as a liquid sweetener. Grind figs, dates, pine nuts, one-third cup the raisins, and two-thirds cup walnuts in food processor or through Champion juicer with blank. Place in large bowl. Knead in all remaining ingredients until well mixed, but do not handle too much. On large platter or tray, mold cake into desired shape. Frost with Queen Elinor Cream Frosting. For best flavor and texture, refrigerate cake four hours or overnight before serving. It can be kept in refrigerator up to one week.

Queen Elinor Cream Frosting

Ingredients

2 cups pitted dates, soaked 1 hour in 1 cup of water
1 cup pine nuts
1 tsp. pure vanilla

To Prepare

Drain dates and save water. Blend dates, pine nuts and vanilla in food processor or blender for three minutes or until smooth, adding a little soak water if necessary. If desired, save remaining soak water for use as a liquid sweetener for up to six weeks.

For best texture, refrigerate frosting at least six hours or overnight before using. For whiter cake, cover with a layer of moist shredded unsweetened coconut after frosting.

The above recipes are from *Sweet Temptations* by Frances Kendall. The book is out of print.

Banana/Coconut/Tahini Cream Pie*

Ingredients

Crust
1 ½ -2 cups pecans
½ cup dates
½ tsp. vanilla

Filling
½ cup dates
2 cups coconut
¼ cup soak water from dates
¼ cup tahini hint of vanilla
6 bananas, sliced

Almond Crème
2 cups almonds, soaked overnight and peeled
1 tsp. vanilla
⅓ cup maple syrup water to cover

To Prepare

Blend crust ingredients with S blade in food processor and put in pie dish

Spread three bananas to cover the crust. Blend all ingredients for filling in food processor and spread over the bananas.

Mix all ingredients for almond crème in blender, adding more water if needed to make a smooth texture. Spread one-half of the almond crème over the filling. Slice last three bananas over the almond crème and top with last half of almond crème.

*This recipe was created by Caroline Carriere and Patricia Schmidt.

Cranberry Salad

Ingredients

1 pound bag of fresh cranberries
3 oranges
3 stalks of celery, chopped fine
1 ½ cups chopped walnuts
½ lemon, juiced
1 cup frozen, unsweetened raspberries
½ fresh pineapple
½ to ¾ cup honey

To Prepare

Grind cranberries and oranges in food processor on pulse. Mix well with remaining ingredients. Can be refrigerated overnight

Mother Knows Best Salad

Ingredients

2 bunches spinach
2 bunches Swiss chard
Spiral carrots
bag of arame, soaked
2-3 onions, diced
4 lemons, juiced tomato
olive oil
Bragg's Aminos
Celtic salt
apple cider vinegar
dill
thyme

To Prepare

Combine all ingredients.

Jade's Sensuous Salmon

Ingredients

4 cups sprouted yellow peas (lentils or garbanzos can be used) 6-8 carrots
2 jalapenos
8-10 cloves garlic
2 stalks celery
4 red onions
8 cloves garlic spices to taste

To Prepare

Put first four ingredients through Champion juicer with the blank. Mince remaining ingredients. Combine all thoroughly.

Sweet Onion Relish

Ingredients

chopped onion to fill serving bowl
2 Tbsp. dill weed
3 tsp. turmeric
2-3 lemons, juiced 1 tsp. Celtic salt
1-2 Tbsp. honey

To Prepare

Mix well. Keeps for 30 days.

Spice It Up!!!

Vegetables	Suggested Flavorings & Seasonings
Asparagus	Caraway seed, lemon juice, mustard seed, sesame seed, tarragon
Beans	Basil, dill seed, unsalted French dressing, lemon juice, marjoram, mint, mustard seed, nutmeg, oregano, sage, savory, sugar, tarragon, thyme
Beets	Allspice, bay leaves, caraway seed, cloves, dill seed, mustard seed, tarragon
Broccoli	Caraway seed, dill seed, lemon butter, mustard seed, oregano, tarragon
Cabbage	Caraway seed, dill seed, mint, mustard seed, dry mustard, nutmeg, poppy seed, savory, thyme, vinegar
Carrots	Allspice, bay leaves, caraway seed, chives, cloves, dill, fennel, ginger, green pepper, mace, marjoram, mint, nutmeg, thyme
Cauliflower	Caraway seed, chives, dill seed, lemon juice, mace, nutmeg, parsley, rosemary, tarragon
Corn	Curry, green pepper
Cucumber	Basil, dill seed, lemon juice, mint, nutmeg, tarragon
Eggplant	Chives, grated onion or garlic, lemon butter, marjoram, oregano, chopped parsley, tarragon
Lettuce salad	Basil, caraway seeds, chives, dill, garlic, lemon, onion, tarragon, thyme, vinegar
Onions	Caraway seed, mustard seed, nutmeg, oregano, red or green pepper, sage, thyme
Peas	Basil, dill, marjoram, mint, oregano, lemon butter, parsley, green pepper, poppy seed, rosemary, sage, savory, thyme

How to Sprout

SOAK　　　DRAIN　　　RINSE　　　DAYS LATER

Almost any seed, grain or legume can be sprouted. Seeds offer a concentrated storehouse of energy and nutrients, held in reserve, ready to burst forth when a suitable environment is offered.

During the sprouting process, vitamins, minerals, proteins ane enzymes are produced at an incredible rate. Vitamin content triples at least. In wheat, vitamin B-complex and vitamin C increase by 600 percent.

Most seeds will yield between 6 and 10 times their weight in sprouts! Sprouts are by far the most economical and nutritious food you can eat. Be sure that the seeds or grains have not been chemically treated. If they have been, the germination rate will drop.

Basically, care of sprouts means keeping them moist and providing adequate aeration and drainage.

Soaking

Put seeds in jar and cover with screen, secure with rubber band or place seeds in sprout bag and put in bowl. Then fill jar or bowl about half-way with lukewarm water, preferably filtered water. Seeds are soaked according to their size. Check your charts for soaking time.

Draining

After the seeds have been soaked, drain off the water. Rinse sprouts with fresh water, pour off; if using bags, dip whole bag in water and hang up to drain. Now let sprouts rest by tilting jar upside down at a 45 degree angle, making sure that the opening allows air in and is not completely covered by the sprouts. A dish rack is useful for this. Keep out of direct sunlight for the first few days.

Rinsing

To rinse, stand the jar upright. Let the water fill the jar. As it does, you will see a ring of foam rise to the top. Let the water overflow and carry the foam away. The foam contains the waste products of the sprouts.

Rinse and drain well two or three times a day. Use cool water. Rinsing is basically making sure sprouts are kept moist.

Harvesting of Sprouts

The outside layers of seeds (hulls) are removed in a process called "harvesting" before eating. Alfalfa, radish, red clover and mung respond well to harvesting.

Fenugreek, sunflower, peas, grains and lentils don't need it.

Place sprouts in a bowl or in the sink and fill with water. The hulls will rise to the surface and the sprouts will sink to the bottom. Scoop off the hulls from the surface and reach underneath the sprouts and pick them out of the water. Place the sprouts back in a jar and drain off excess water.

Alfalfa, radish and cabbage sprouts need to be set in indirect sunlight after five days so that they can start manufacturing chlorophyll. Sprouts are most tender when young, and they refrigerate well.

Sprouted Wheat

Living, sprouted wheat contains the eight essential amino acids or proteins needed by the body in an easily assimilable form. Sprouted wheat also contains vitamin E and more vitamin C than an orange.

Wheat sprouts are used to make rejuvelac, blended with raisins to make cereals, in salads and sunbaked bread. It is important to use as a winter food for cold climates.

Alfalfa Sprouts

The "queen of sprouts" sends its plant roots as deep as fifty feet into the earth to gather trace minerals from the soil. Sprouts are rich in amino acids, minerals, enzymes, chlorophyll and vitamins A, B, C, D, E, F and K. The fiber is easily digested and is a wonderful intestinal cleanser. Note: According to Dr. Andrew Weil, alfalfa sprouts contain canavanine, a toxin that can harm the immune system. Therefore, I would suggest that chronically ill individuals not use alfalfa sprouts and other legumes, but use non-leguminous sprouts such as fenugreek, radish, broccoli, cabbage, buckwheat, etc.

Mung Bean Sprouts

Mung sprouts are rich in vitamins A, C and B-complex. They are a complete food when mixed with alfalfa. They quadruple their vitamin content during the sprouting process. These beans are sprouted best in the dark and under pressure.

Lentil Sprouts

These are some of the most ancient beans on earth. Cooked lentils can be acid-forming and cause flatulence. Lentils are alkaline when sprouted. They are rich in vitamins, minerals (especially) and amino acids.

Fenugreek Sprouts

These sprouts are effective cleansers of the blood, liver and kidney. Fenugreek is an herb and has been used for centuries in the Middle East as a tea to clear away mucous in the bronchioles. They are a great lymphatic cleanser and natural deodorant. They have the very pleasant fragrance of maple syrup . . . and you will, too.

Radish Sprouts

These sprouts are blood cleansers and heat producers. They are nice for providing warmth in the diet. They are hot, so use moderately. Also used as a natural diuretic.

Chickpea Sprouts

Chickpea sprouts are a complete protein and much more easily digested than when they are cooked.

They make a delicious raw Hummus.

Rejuvelac

The value of rejuvelac and fermented foods in the daily diet

A. Helps cleanse the intestinal tract.
   1. Lactic acid destroys harmful intestinal bacteria.
   2. Babies being breast-fed within the first 48 hours of their life receive a sufficient amount of lactobacillus bifidus, a friendly bacteria culture in the intestine. However, this culture can be destroyed by introducing unnatural, cooked and dead foods.

B. Developing a healthy strain of the friendly bacteria, such as lactobacillus, saccharomyces, and aspergillus oryzae (all of which are found in rejuvelac) strengthens resistance to foreign bacteria in the event of international travel.

C. Supplies nutritional elements such as protein, carbohydrates, dextrines, saccharins, phosphate, and vitamins.

D. Enzymes are the catalysts of life. Dr. Ann Wigmore believes "life begins with catalysts and continues only through them." These enzymes break down food substances to simpler forms. Our bodies can only use the nutrients in this fully broken-down state. Cooking can destroy these enzymes, and create bad food combinations will slow down or stop their action, causing incomplete digestion and putrefaction in the colon. Eating live foods packed with enzymes will ensure a strong enzymatic capacity for efficient digestion and a youthful body.

E. Contains many enzymes, one if which is amylase, which breaks down glucose, starch, and glycogens and aspergillus, which is a common digestive aid.

F. The proteins and starches contained in rejuvelac are predigested. They are broken down to their simplest forms — amino acids and simple sugars. This makes the nutrients immediately available for assimilation, even for those with weak digestive systems. Rejuvelac is instant energy — the "Gatorade" of the health-conscious.

G. Contains the full complex of B-vitamins, which aids in the calming and rebuilding of nerves.

H. Helps with constipation problems.

I. Supples valuable liquid to the body for flushing out of toxins and proper temperature balance.

J. Helps to have friendly flora in intestine. A healthy colon manufactures B-12.

How to make rejuvelac

1. Soak ½ cup wheat seeds (or rye or millet or any grain) 10-12 hours (hard or soft varieties will work).
2. Drain. Let sprout for one day (rinse twice per day).
3. Grind seed in wheatgrass juicer or meat grinder or blend in a Vita-Mix with equal amounts of water
4. Put one cup ground seed sprouts into a gallon jar and fill with purified water.
5. Let stand at room temperature, stirring two times each day for three to four days.

(**Note**: Fermentation time — and therefore taste — will vary according to temperature of room.) Experiment for yourself!

Dr. Ann Wigmore, creator of rejuvelac, advised to start using rejuvelac gradually, drinking 8 ounces of rejuvelac and working up to three quarts daily.

Health Benefits of Some Vegetables Used With Raw/Living Foods

Broccoli	Contains anti-cancer properties. Use daily along with cabbage, parsley, celery and Kale.
Cabbage	Cleans the whole system. Use daily, juiced or in salads. Cabbage is known to be helpful with stomach ulcers.
Carrot	Good for rheumatism, helps to lower blood pressure, clears the skin and contains many nourishing salts and organic sulfur. Use celery often, preferably organically grown, for usually celery is heavily treated with pesticides.
Chicory	Use for gout and rheumatism.
Cucumber	Good for high blood pressure, arthritis and for the skin.
Dandelion	Good for diabetic conditions. Also good for the blood.
Fennel	Stimulates and aids digestion. Add to salads. The herb is calming for those who are high-strung.
Garlic	A powerful antiseptic. Good for stomach and heart. Helps with cholesterol.
Horseradish	Helps liver work better. Stimulates the appetite. Has antiseptic qualities; kills bacteria and germs. Add to dressings, tomato juice and seed cheese.
Lovage	Resembles celery. Aids digestion and helps kidneys function properly. The root can be grated and added to soups. Leaves are used in salads.
Marjoram	Good for the stomach and nervous complaints. It has preserving qualities and is a strong disinfectant. Use with a light hand, for it is bitter — one-half teaspoon for four people. Use with mixed greens and beans.

Nettle	Helps to keep the system healthy and blood pure. It is alkaline and a solvent for uric acid. Helpful for rheumatism. Rich in iron. Gather young green tops.
Onion	Contains free uncrystallized sugar, starch, alkaline salts, sulfur and other valuable food substances. Note: Cut onions, if left lying around, draw all kinds of germs. Do not save cut onions unless wrapped.
Peas	Basil, dill, marjoram, mint, oregano, lemon butter, parsley, green pepper, poppy seed, rosemary, sage, savory, thyme
Oregano	Use the same as marjoram.
Parsley	High in anti-cancer properties. Helps to keep the system clear and disease-free. Use daily in salads, dressings or sauces. Fresh is best.
Radish	Good for purifying the blood. Eases previous exhaustion, sinus congestion and catarrh. A natural antiseptic protection from infection.
Rosemary	A sweet herb that is good for nervous headaches and shakiness.
Spinach	A great source of chlorophyll. Contains high anti-oxidant properties. Do not cook spinach, for this releases oxalic acid.
Turnip	Provides a lot of nutrition. Do not use if you have a weak digestive system.

Note: Parsley, sage, rosemary and thyme fight cancer. Parsley has lutein and zeaxanthan to fight age-related macular degeneration. Carnosol in rosemary may prevent cholesterol oxidation, and the flavones in thyme may help prevent blood clotting. Use in salads, soups or dressings.

Living Foods Milk Alternatives

by Nina Petrellis

Why switch to vegetable-quality, living-food milk?

Today's commercial cow's milk is of a highly questionable quality, and some authorities have said that it is unfit for human consumption. There are many important reasons to consider. The first compelling reason is that much pollution finds its way into cow's milk, such as the many drugs used to treat the sick animals. These drugs include:

- antibiotics
- hormones, including rBGH, also known as recombinant bovine growth hormone, said to cause breast cancer in women
- cortisone
- pesticides, fungicides, and herbicides present in the cow's food and hazardous environmental pollutants.

Another issue to consider is that human beings are the only animal species that drinks the milk of another species. Many modern mothers have been convinced that human milk is replaceable by infant formula, most often made from cow's milk. Human mother's milk is a dynamic, living, whole food designed by nature to best support the growth and development of a human baby. Formula, on the other hand, is a denatured, synthetic milk substitute. It contains significantly higher proportions of protein than mother's milk, many pollutants and none of the factors that fresh, live mother's milk confers to the baby for building the immune system.

Mother's milk is designed to promote the development of the human brain and intelligence. Cow's milk cannot do this, either. Formula is made of cooked and synthetic proteins, fats, vitamins and minerals, all of which promote an acid condition and diseases later in life. Many people in this age of artificial, mass-produced, denatured foods and beverages were also formula fed, and we now see an increase in many degenerative diseases.

Is it any wonder that so many people suffer from allergies and so many degenerative diseases today? Scientists tell us that there is a direct link between the drinking of cow's milk and allergies, intestinal disorders, lactose intolerance, bed-wetting, constipation, infant colic, high cholesterol and many forms of cancer.

Even if milk is organically produced, it is still meant to nourish a baby calf in its natural raw form. A calf develops very quickly physically, with low intelligence. Cow's milk is perfect for the calf's development.

Once cow's milk is pasteurized, it is a dead food and its living enzymes are destroyed, its protein is deranged and its vitamins and minerals are greatly reduced. If pasteurized milk is fed to calves, they will die in a very short period of time. We have to ask what the effects are on people.

What is the answer?

Welcome whole, living foods, vegetable-quality milk! With inventiveness, any nuts, seeds or grain can be healthfully prepared into a satisfying milk. Living foods milk can be used in any way cow's milk can be used.

Nut milks make excellent and digestible drinks. Their richness and degree of sweetness can be altered to taste. The milk recipes can be made into the base for living food soups, smoothies or sauces, besides being delicious and nourishing as a drink by themselves.

Almonds and sesame seeds are the best choices from a nutritional standpoint, but other seeds and nuts can be used according to taste and imagination! Try making them individually and in combinations and see what appeals to you.

Living foods milk can be sweetened with a variety of natural sweeteners, including dates, raisins, raw honey, maple syrup, stevia or vanilla.

A good ratio of nuts or seeds to water is one part nuts to three to six cups of water.

Almonds may be soaked and then quickly blanched to ease digestion. After soaking nuts for 24 hours to deactivate the enzyme inhibitors, drop them into a pan of just boiled water. Remove them after 10 seconds and place in a bowl of cold water. Then pinch each almond to release them from their skins.

After blending the seeds and nuts, it is important to strain the milk through a fine mesh strainer. Press the pulp with the back of a spoon to extract all the milk, or squeeze it through a cheesecloth. The pulp can be added to dehydrator cookies, natural halvah, soups, dressings or seed cheeses.

The following pages contain recipes to get you started.

Dr. Ann Wigmore's Nut and Seed Milk

Ingredients

- ⅓ cup of any nut or seed: almond, sesame, cashew, sunflower, Brazil nut, walnut or pecan
- 1 cup pure water
- 2 tsp. raw honey (optional); or a banana, apple, or pear may be added for sweetness
- 1-2 drops pure vanilla extract

Optional Ingredients:

For a mineral boost, add c tsp. of kelp powder or ¼ tsp. dulse. Two to four pitted dates may be added as a sweetener per one-half cup of seeds or nuts.

To Prepare

Choose one nut or seed or a combination.

Method #1: Grind dry seeds in a coffee grinder or grain mill. Place ground seeds (or nuts) and remaining ingredients into a blender and blend all to a milk consistency. Strain through a fine mesh strainer, pressing out all the milk and place in a jar. Use immediately. Will keep one or two days in the refrigerator.

Method #2: Soak the nuts and seeds for 24 hours. Then discard the soak water. Place the seeds or nuts in the blender, adding pure water in stages to thoroughly grind the seeds.

More water may be added for a thinner milk. Add sweetener to taste. Strain and store as above.

Soaking makes the seeds and nuts alkaline forming and deactivates their naturally occurring enzyme inhibitors and greatly increases their nutritional profile.

Dr. Ann's Wheat Milk

Ingredients

½ cup 2-day wheat sprouts
1 cup pure water
1 Tbsp. unrefined maple syrup
3 dates or figs (optional)

To Prepare

Put the water in the blender and gradually blend in the wheat sprouts while the motor is on. Blend in the sweeteners to taste. Strain through a fine mesh strainer. Makes 8 ounces.

Malted Wheat Milk

Ingredients

1 ½ cups 2-day wheat sprouts
1 cup pure water
3 dates, pitted
1 ripe banana, sliced
2 Tbsp. carob powder

To Prepare

Blend the water with the sprouts as above. Pour through a fine mesh strainer and return the liquid to the blender. Add the dates, banana and carob powder. Blend again. Makes 12 ounces.

Variations

Other sprouted grains can be used such as quinoa, kamut, amaranth, millet, spelt or unsteamed oat groats.

The Benefits of Raw/Living Foods

1. Have additional energy and endurance for a more satisfying life and be able to carry out activities.
2. Living foods, rich in enzymes, will help your body detoxify itself from toxicity in a first step, then to rejuvenate the cells and organs.
3. By giving your body highly nutritive food, your immune system will be able to fight infections and diseases in a more powerful way.
4. Living food is a preventive means from illness and unnecessary aging, physically and mentally.
5. Stress factors can be reduced naturally and quickly because living food helps to calm the nerve cells as they are purely nourished with LIVE ENERGY from foods free from additives, preservatives, pesticides and chemicals — all of which may counteract the ability of the mind to relax.
6. Living food clears the mind to allow the flow of creative thinking and provides the brain with oxygen, giving your brain clean breathing (thinking) space.
7. Living food is a means to quickly prepare a balanced meal, especially for the busy business person and/or career homemaker. Living food is healthy fast food!
8. Living food provides relief from concerns regarding "unknown hazards" in regard to additives, preservatives or pesticides, which need to be considered even from our store-bought organic foods. Quality control is in your hands when you provide yourself with your own living foods, home-grown indoors! The loving energy and care you put into providing yourself with your own sprouts, greens, composting, etc., is returned to you in the food you eat.
9. Living food is a means of preventing illness and unnecessary aging, physically and mentally.

Having a "Natural" Ball at Holiday Times or Special Occasions

Menu

Mock Turkey 96

Holiday Dressing 102

Mock Potato Salad 50

Mock Cranberry Sauce 57

Apple Blossom Salad 59

Apple Pie 85

Sweet Potato Pie .... 81 or 83

Menu Planning Guidelines

- Breakfast should be a light meal because your digestive system may not be awake or ready to handle heavy foods. Avoid fatty foods for breakfast.
- Blended smoothies, watermelon juice, nut and seed milks and cereals are good choices for breakfast that will give you energy without overburdening your digestive system.
- All nuts and seeds should be soaked overnight before use, to activate the enzymes.
- Make sure that you add some "Living" food to your breakfasts. Enzymes are very important for digestion. Sprouted foods contain a lot of enzymes.
- Flax seed is one of the richest sources of omega-3 fatty acids, which are excellent for your heart, arteries, nervous system, are wonderful for elimination and the list goes on and on. Make sure that you get 1 to 2 Tbsp. every day. Grind them and blend them in your smoothies and dressings, sprinkle them over your smoothies, cereals, and salads, soup, etc.
- Be careful or avoid sugars and natural sweeteners if you have cancer, diabetes, or candida related problem. Banana is the fruit that contain the most sugar. Dry fruits are extremely rich in sugars. Grains (bread, pasta, etc.) turn into sugar also, Granny Smith apples contains the least sugar.

Purée — Any fruit can be blended and eaten. A ripe banana can be added for more sweetness. Apple also lends body to purées.

Fruit smoothies can include any of these items:

For body: Apple and/or banana or watermelon.

To add living vitamins and enzymes: sprouted grains such as wheat, rye and kamut.

Liquid: Pure water or fruit juice, or rejuvelac (note: rejuvelac acts as a preservative for vitamins and enzymes and adds more nutrition to the smoothie).

For calories and a smooth texture, add: avocado (always blend as the last item. Do not over-blend.)

To add protein, minerals, or for a different texture, use: sunflower seed sprouts (high in complete protein), pumpkin seed sprouts (high in zinc), soaked almonds (rich in calcium), ground hulled white sesame (especially rich in calcium and magnesium) and old fashioned rolled oats (good source of fiber).

Seasonings: (Note: these are optional and most people should avoid these while detoxifying) cinnamon, cloves, allspice, pumpkin spice, ginger, cardamom, nutmeg, etc.

Raw Foods and the Biggest Myth Ever

by Bob McCauley Author, *Achieving Great Health*

The biggest nutritional myth that has been perpetuated through the centuries and remains well established to this day is that a diet comprised mostly of cooked foods is healthy.

As a species, we have only eaten cooked foods for a very short period of time. To put it into perspective with an analogy, if we started walking and did not stop for three days, that is how long we have been living on a raw food diet. If we then took seven more steps, that is how long we have been cooking our food. We are the only species in the world that cooks our food and we are the only species that gets sick except for the pets we domesticate and put on a processed food diet.

The first thing we need to understand about cooked foods is that they are an addiction. There are healthy and unhealthy addictions. Cooked foods are an unhealthy addiction because they are detrimental to the body for several reasons. When we do something strictly for pleasure and not for any other reason and we can't stop doing it, it should be considered an unhealthy addiction. To say that eating raw foods is an addiction is a misnomer because the nutrients in raw foods are required by the body in order for it to be healthy; therefore, raw foods should not be considered an addiction.

It should not be stated lightly that cooked foods prematurely age the body and lead to all chronic disease. Once we recognize this, we can begin to treat our addiction to them. It is difficult to admit any addiction to anything, let alone something that has been at the core of our lives since we can remember. We are taught that disease is inevitable and strikes at random. It is difficult to remove an addiction from our lives. All addictions are physical, psychological and/or emotional and, therefore, are worldly in nature. Thus, removing worldly addictions from our lives is a spiritual event that raises us higher. We all have certain foods that we like and have a hard time avoiding. With me, those foods are pizza and chocolate. But I find that the more I stay away from them, the easier they are to avoid. Like anything else that we are addicted to, we must completely stay away from those substances because the temptation to go back to them could be too strong to resist. A person can jump into raw foods with both feet, end their cooked food addiction cold turnkey and do well. But that is an exception to the norm. Most of us need to transform slowly into the raw-food life and this should be done by increasing our intake of raw foods and decreasing our intake of cooked foods each day.

We spend our childhood being conditioned to eat cooked foods. Raw foods are all but shunned for the most part. Even in the womb, we receive nutrients in a diminished capacity from a mother's diet of cooked, denatured foods. Therefore, the natural state of the body is never realized. We spend our lives in a body that is completely different from the body that nature intended us to have; something like an alter-body like that of an alter-ego. It exists in a way that nature did not intend it to exist. A body fed mostly cooked foods is different in many ways from the natural body. The body that is fed cooked, denatured foods is a denatured body. Its immune system is weak. Its organs produce diminished quantities of enzymes. The pH of the denatured body is usually acid, therefore abnormal. The denatured body's normal balance is at greater risk of destabilization, leading to a cascading effect of health problems, which is why doctors sometimes have difficulty diagnosing what disease a person actually has. Warnings of all kinds manifest themselves in the body of the cooked foodist. Acid reflux, joint pain, bowel problems are amongst the first to appear.

A body that is fed cooked foods is like a building that is designed to be constructed and maintained using one particular set of materials, but another set of materials is actually used in it. Thus, the entire structure — in this case the body — is constructed of inferior materials that are destined to lead to maintenance problems, meaning chronic diseases of every kind.

Cooked foods unnaturally and prematurely deform the body. In extreme cases, they make people chair-ridden, even bed-ridden by the time they are in their fifties. Death in these cases is slow and agonizing. It becomes for some a living death with intermittent trips to the hospital as they slowly waste away over a period of many years. And with each return from the hospital, the body is a little more diminished and less likely to fully recover as drugs are prescribed one on top of another.

The craving for cooked foods that is conditioned into the mind and boy itself has no connection whatsoever with the actual nutritional demands of the body. The appetite of the cooked foodist is insatiable because the body's nutritional needs are never entirely met. This leads to gluttony and other eating disorders that simply are not found in the wild. A bear or bird does not suffer from acid reflux or obesity. A raw foodist does not have these types of conditions. In fact, there is no evidence of chronic disease in the wild of any kind. For instance, no one has ever shot a deer, taken it home, cut it open and found it full of cancer. All addictions are outgrowths of unnatural circumstances. Disease itself is NOT a natural part of the human condition.

A chronic cooked-food died manifests itself by grossly disfiguring the body as it ages. Thighs begin to look like cottage cheese, bellies become sacks of flab as do chins, arms and breasts. Chronic lack of exercise adds to the grotesque features of bodies deprived of the enzymes that are found only in raw foods.

When you are sick, your doctor prescribes drugs for your problems. The chances of your arthritis being cured at any time in your life from that or any other visit to the doctor's office are zero.

Drugs don't cure chronic disease; they treat symptoms and outer manifestations, but they do not rid the body of disease. Disease is opportunist and springs to life in a body living on a diet of cooked foods, which deposit small amounts of acid waste in the joints of the body, which have manifested itself as rheumatoid or osteoarthritis.

The raw food diet is 100% successful in preventing and even curing the body of all disease each and every time it is tried. Many will ask why they never heard this before if all this is true. I don't know the answer to that question, but now you know the truth. When it comes to health, raw foods rule!

Reprinted by permission. Bob McCauley is owner of The Watershed Wellness Center, 6439 W. Saginaw Hwy, Lansing, Michigan 48917. www.watershed.net. Bob's book, *Achieving Great Health,* has been translated into Chinese.

Creative Health Institute
112 West Union City Road
Union City, MI 49094
517-278-6260
www.creativehealthinstitute.com

Useful Contacts and References for a Raw Lifestyle

Raw Food Websites:

Creative Health Institute (CHI): www.creativehealthinstitute.com. Teaching Dr. Ann Wigmore's Living Foods Lifestyle program for more than 30 years.

Raw Family: www.rawfamily.com. Home page of the Boutenko family.

Living and raw foods: www.living-foods.com. Huge online community; great bulletin board.

Raw Vegan Radio: www.rawveganradio.com. Fantastic new site with free raw interviews to download. We Like it Raw: www.welikeitraw.com. Information-rich site on all things raw.

Raw Food Planet: www.rawfoodplanet.com. Worldwide raw lifestyle directory.

Recommended Reading

Boutenko, Victoria. *Green For Life*. An impressive and much-appreciated work on the importance of greens. Raw Family Publishing, 2000.

Cousins, Gabriel. *Rainbow Green Live-Food Cuisine*. The ultimate raw-food handbook — incredible, in- depth work.

Wigmore, Ann. *Rebuild Your Health*. Second Edition. The complete Living Foods Lifestyle program. Ann Wigmore Foundation, 1991.

Wigmore, Ann. *Why Suffer*. An autobiography.

Wolfe, David. *Sun food Diet Success System*. 6th Edition.

Sprouting for Wellness

Country Life National Foods (ask for OG)
800-456-7694
P.O. Box 489
Pullman, MI 49450

Frontier (ask for OG)
800-669-3275
3021 78th St., P.O. Box 299
Norway, IA 52318

Harvest Health Foods
616-245-6268
1944 Eastern SE
Grand Rapids, MI 49507

Harvest Time Natural Foods (ask for OG)
800-628-8736
3565 South Onondaga Rd.
Eaton Rapids, MI 48827

Sun Organic Farm (OG)
888-269-9888
P.O. Box 2429
Valley Center, CA 92082

Tiensvold Farm (OG)
308-327-3135
HC 81 Box 22
Rushville, NE 69360

Detoxify & Rejuvenate

The Assembly of Yahweh Wellness Center

A raw- and living-foods holistic health and training center located in the wooded farmland of south central Michigan

Monthly one- and two-week resident health programs

We also offer evening food preparation and other health classes.

And we offer rest and relaxation retreats for people already familiar with a raw/living foods lifestyle.

Our facility is located on 80 acres of lush, green, wooded farmland just south of Lansing, Michigan. Come away from the hustle of city life and take along, safe walks with us under the trees on quiet country roads.

We provide a homey, family-style atmosphere with comfortable private and semi-private rooms, with individual or shared bathrooms. Our main house has five comfortable beds, and there is plenty of land for tents and self-contained campers.

We have sprouts, wild greens, regular organic produce and all the indoor greens and grasses of the Ann Wigmore program.

Our program director is Hiawatha Cromer, who held the same position for eight years at Creative Health Institute in Union City, Michigan. We will train you in the easy-to-make, yet very healthy foods and show you how to do the inner cleansing methods of Dr. Ann's program. You can then see for yourself how it works for you. And we'll help you set up a program you can do at home.

We also have morning stretching classes, relaxation exercises, outdoor waling and lymphatic cleansing on our mini-trampolines, plus a library and health and personal enjoyment videos.

Our health center is non-denominational, but in following with Dr. Ann Wigmore's understanding, we encourage our guests to have, or to develop, some kind of personal spiritual orientation because it is part of a holistic, healthy life.

For a pleasant, healthful learning experience, just start by giving us a call, and we'll fill you in on the details.

7911 Columbia Highway • Eaton Rapids, MI 48827 • 517-663-1637

Take M-99 south from Lansing or I-69. Go about 7 miles south of I-69 and turn right at the blinking light of Columbia Hwy. Go 3 miles to the 3rd stop sign at Gunnel. Cross Gunnel onto the dirt road, go a couple hundred feet, and turn right into our driveway. From Eaton Rapids, go north on M-99 7 miles to Columbia.

Printed in the USA
CPSIA information can be obtained
at www.ICGtesting.com
LVHW111254030823
753911LV00001B/81